CHICKEN
AND POULTRY

GOOD HOUSEKEEPING
STEP-BY-STEP COOKERY

CHICKEN AND POULTRY

Guild Publishing/Ebury Press
LONDON

This edition published 1984 by
Book Club Associates
By arrangement with Ebury Press

Consultant editor: Jeni Wright
Editor: Nicole Foster
Design by Mike Leaman
Drawings by John Woodcock
Photographs by Peter Myers

Cover photograph: Chicken Marengo (page 83),
Traditional Roast Chicken (page 121)

Filmset by Advanced Filmsetters (Glasgow) Ltd

Printed and bound in Italy by
New Interlitho, S.p.a., Milan

CONTENTS

COOKERY NOTES

Follow either metric or imperial measures for the recipes in this book as they are not inter-changeable. Sets of spoon measures are available in both metric and imperial size to give accurate measurement of small quantities. All spoon measures are level unless otherwise stated. When measuring milk we have used the exact conversion of 568 ml (1 pint).
* Size 4 eggs should be used except when otherwise stated.
† Granulated sugar is used un-less otherwise stated.
● Plain flour is used unless otherwise stated.

OVEN TEMPERATURE CHART

°C	°F	Gas mark
110	225	$\frac{1}{4}$
130	250	$\frac{1}{2}$
140	275	1
150	300	2
170	325	3
180	350	4
190	375	5
200	400	6
220	425	7
230	450	8
240	475	9

KEY TO SYMBOLS

1.00* Indicates minimum preparation and cooking times in hours and minutes. They do not include prepared items in the list of ingredients; calcu-lated times apply only to the method. An asterisk * indicates extra time should be allowed, so check the note below symbols.

Chef's hats indicate degree of difficulty of a recipe: no hat means it is straightforward; one hat slightly more complicated; two hats indicates that it is for more advanced cooks.

£ Indicates a recipe which is good value for money; £ £ indicates an expensive recipe. No £ sign indicates an inexpensive recipe.

✳ Indicates that a recipe will freeze. If there is no symbol, the recipe is unsuitable for freezing. An asterisk * indicates special freezer instructions so check the note immediately below the symbols.

309 cals Indicates calories per serving, including any sugges-tions (e.g. cream, to serve) given in the ingredients.

METRIC CONVERSION SCALE

LIQUID			SOLID		
Imperial	Exact conversion	Recommended ml	Imperial	Exact conversion	Recommended g
$\frac{1}{4}$ pint	142 ml	150 ml	1 oz	28.35 g	25 g
$\frac{1}{2}$ pint	284 ml	300 ml	2 oz	56.7 g	50 g
1 pint	568 ml	600 ml	4 oz	113.4 g	100 g
1$\frac{1}{2}$ pints	851 ml	900 ml	8 oz	226.8 g	225 g
1$\frac{3}{4}$ pints	992 ml	1 litre	12 oz	340.2 g	350 g
For quantities of 1$\frac{3}{4}$ pints and over, litres and fractions of a litre have been used.			14 oz	397.0 g	400 g
			16 oz (1 lb)	453.6 g	450 g
			1 kilogram (kg) equals 2.2 lb.		

CHICKEN AND POULTRY

Versatility is the key note of this book. Never before has there been such a varied collection of unusual and imaginative recipes for chicken and poultry. Some exotic and new, perfect for special occasions, others classic, traditional and everyday, but all equally delicious and simple to follow with our step-by-step methods and helpful illustrations. Each recipe has its own full-colour photograph to tempt you to cook, and there is even a menu suggestion for each dish to help you decide which vegetables to serve or whether wine or beer is the most suitable drink.

In the tinted section at the back of the book, you will see a collection of useful information and basic recipes. This is to help you with all the different aspects of chicken and poultry cooking. Apart from recipes for stocks, gravies, stuffings and sauces, there is information on methods of cooking, from simple roasting and grilling to the less familiar brick cookery and stir-frying.

Choosing poultry can be a problem if you are not sure what to look for—we give you tips about buying, storing and thawing to help you make the right decision. And for all those tricky techniques such as trussing, boning, jointing and skinning, there is a special section which takes you step-by-step through every stage.

Soups

You'll be amazed how many deliciously different soups can be made with chicken and poultry. This chapter draws ideas and inspiration from all round the world. Chunky chowder and gumbo from America, delicate lemon-flavoured chicken soup with rice from Greece, substantial soups from Scotland and Belgium, plus a soup brimfull of exotic ingredients from China. They're all beautifully simple for you to make, and there's something for every taste and every occasion.

Avgolemono

0.35	🍴	98 cals

Serves 4

1.5 litres (2½ pints) homemade
　chicken stock (see page 157)
50 g (2 oz) long grain rice
2 egg yolks
100 ml (4 fl oz) freshly squeezed
　lemon juice
salt and freshly ground pepper
lemon slices and coriander sprigs,
　to garnish

1 Bring the stock to the boil in a
large saucepan. Add the rice
and simmer uncovered for 20
minutes until the rice is cooked.

2 Put the egg yolks and lemon
juice in a bowl and whisk in a
few tablespoonfuls of the hot
chicken stock.

3 Pour the mixture gradually
into the pan of stock, whisking
all the time. Simmer gently without boiling for a few minutes, then
add salt and pepper to taste.

4 Pour into warmed individual
bowls and garnish each one
with a lemon slice and a sprig of
coriander. Serve hot.

Menu Suggestion
Serve this tangy, lemon-flavoured
soup with hot pitta bread before a
main course of chicken or lamb.

CREAM OF CHICKEN SOUP

| 0.45 | ✳* | 120 cals |

* freeze without the cream

Serves 4

45 ml (3 tbsp) flour
150 ml ($\frac{1}{4}$ pint) milk
1.1 litres (2 pints) homemade
    chicken stock (see page 157)
100 g (4 oz) cooked chicken, diced
salt and freshly ground pepper
5 ml (1 tsp) lemon juice
pinch of grated nutmeg
30 ml (2 tbsp) single cream
croûtons and parsley sprigs, to
    garnish

1 In a large bowl, blend the flour with a little of the milk until it makes a smooth cream.

2 Bring the stock to the boil, then, stir it into the blended mixture. Return to the pan and simmer gently for 20 minutes.

3 Stir in the chicken, seasoning, lemon juice and nutmeg. Mix the rest of the milk with the cream and stir in. Reheat without boiling.

4 Taste and adjust seasoning, then pour into warmed individual soup bowls. Sprinkle with croûtons and parsley sprigs.

Menu Suggestion
Serve this smooth, rich soup with warmed bridge rolls, before a main course of plain roast or grilled meat.

CHICKEN AND SWEETCORN CHOWDER

1.45 ✳* 331 cals

* freeze after step 4

Serves 6

1.6 kg (3½ lb) chicken
1 litre (1¾ pints) water
salt and freshly ground pepper
1 stick of celery, roughly chopped
1 parsley sprig
1 medium onion, skinned and
   roughly chopped
1 bay leaf
10 peppercorns
two 335-g (11.8-oz) cans sweetcorn,
   drained
6 hard-boiled eggs
45 ml (3 tbsp) chopped fresh
   parsley
150 ml (5 fl oz) single cream, to
   serve

1 Place the chicken in a large saucepan with the water, salt, celery, parsley sprig, onion, bay leaf and peppercorns.

2 Bring to the boil and simmer gently for 1–1½ hours until the chicken is completely tender.

3 When cooked, remove the chicken from the pan and cut the meat into large bite-size pieces. Discard skin and bones.

4 Strain the chicken stock, return it to the saucepan and add the chicken flesh and sweetcorn and simmer for about 5 minutes.

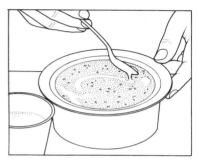

5 Chop the hard-boiled eggs. Add to the soup with the chopped parsley and salt and pepper to taste. Heat through gently, then pour into warmed individual bowls.

6 Swirl cream into each portion and serve the chicken and sweetcorn chowder immediately.

Menu Suggestion
This is a substantial meal-in-itself soup. Serve for a warming supper with garlic bread or French bread and butter, and a sharp, hard cheese such as Farmhouse Cheddar.

CHICKEN AND SWEETCORN CHOWDER

Chowder is a traditional American dish, which originally described thick and chunky fish soups. Nowadays the term is used more loosely and a chowder can be made from a variety of ingredients as long as the finished dish is a cross between a soup and a stew. Juicy, yellow sweetcorn is a common addition to many chowders.

If time is short, you can make a quick chicken chowder by using ready-cooked chicken, skinned, boned and cut into pieces. Simmer them in 900 ml (1½ pints) stock (made from a cube if necessary), with the vegetables and seasonings in the recipe above for 20 minutes. Drain, discarding the vegetables and seasonings and simmer the chicken pieces and stock with the sweetcorn for 5 minutes, then follow the recipe exactly as from step 5.

CHICKEN AND PRAWN GUMBO

0.45	£ £	219–273 cals

Serves 8–10

50 g (2 oz) streaky bacon, rinded and chopped

2 garlic cloves, skinned and finely chopped

1 large onion, skinned and finely chopped

15 ml (1 tbsp) flour

2 tomatoes, skinned and chopped

1 green pepper, cored, seeded and finely sliced

1 bay leaf

1.1 litres (2 pints) chicken stock

175 g (6 oz) long grain rice

225 g (8 oz) okra

450 g (1 lb) cooked chicken, diced

450 g (1 lb) peeled prawns

few drops of Tabasco sauce

few drops of Worcestershire sauce

salt and freshly ground pepper

chopped fresh parsley, to garnish

1 In a large saucepan, cook the bacon gently in its own fat for 2–3 minutes until transparent. Add the garlic and onion and fry gently for about 7 minutes until they are golden.

2 Sprinkle in the flour. Stir well, cook for 1–2 minutes, then remove from the heat.

3 Add the tomatoes and green pepper with the bay leaf and stock. Stir well, return to the heat and bring to the boil. Cover and simmer for 20 minutes. Add the rice and boil for 10 minutes more.

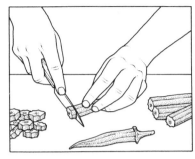

4 Trim the okra and slice evenly into rings. Add to the gumbo with the chicken and prawns, then add the Tabasco and Worcestershire sauces with salt and pepper to taste.

5 Simmer for 10 minutes or until heated through. Ladle the gumbo into a warmed soup tureen and serve sprinkled with chopped fresh parsley.

Menu Suggestion
A hot and spicy soup for an informal lunch or supper party. Serve with warmed bread rolls or hot herb bread.

CHICKEN AND PRAWN GUMBO

Gumbo is the American term for okra, which is sometimes also known as "ladies fingers". Okra is also a common ingredient in Greek cookery, and its slightly gelatinous quality when cooked is used to thicken soups and stews.

Okra can also be served as a vegetable accompaniment: trim, then simmer for 5 minutes, drain and top with melted butter or a hollandaise sauce.

JEWISH CHICKEN SOUP WITH DUMPLINGS

1.45 ✳* 190 cals

* freeze soup without the dumplings

Serves 6

1.1–1.4 kg (2½–3 lb) chicken, skinned

1 medium onion, skinned and
   chopped

1 litre (1¾ pints) chicken stock

350 g (12 oz) carrots, peeled and
   sliced

salt and freshly ground pepper

100 g (4 oz) celery with leaves,
   chopped

For the dumplings

75 g (3 oz) matzo meal

120 ml (4½ fl oz) water

1 egg, beaten

salt

1 Put the chicken, onion, stock, carrots, salt and pepper into a large saucepan and bring to the boil. Reduce the heat, cover and simmer for about 1 hour, until the chicken is tender. Remove the chicken and leave to cool.
Strain the stock into a saucepan and heat to simmering.

2 Meanwhile, make the dumplings. Mix together the matzo meal, water, egg and salt.

3 Shape the mixture into tiny dumplings with your hands. Add the dumplings and celery to the simmering soup. Cook gently for about 20 minutes until the dumplings are cooked.

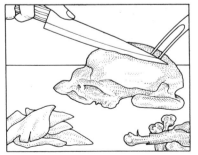

4 Carve the chicken off the bones. Cut the meat into small chunks, stir into the soup and heat through. Taste and adjust seasoning. Pour into warmed soup bowls or a tureen and serve immediately.

Menu Suggestion
A filling soup for a meal with a light main course. Serve on its own or with bread such as poppyseed plait.

JEWISH CHICKEN SOUP WITH DUMPLINGS

This traditional Jewish recipe is topped with tasty dumplings made of matzo meal. Matzo is the main ingredient of Passover cookery, and it is used to make a variety of dishes such as un-leavened bread, matzo pancakes and sweetened fritters which are accompanied with fruit.

COCK-A-LEEKIE SOUP

| 1.15 | ✳ | 91 cals |

Serves 6

15 g (½ oz) butter or margarine
275–350 g (10–12 oz) chicken
   (1 large or 2 small chicken
   portions)
350 g (12 oz) leeks, trimmed
1.1 litres (2 pints) chicken stock
1 bouquet garni
salt and freshly ground pepper
6 prunes, stoned
parsley sprigs, to garnish

1 Melt the fat in a large saucepan and fry the chicken quickly until golden on all sides.

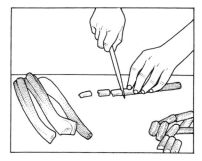

2 Cut the white part of the leeks into four lengthways and chop into 2.5-cm (1-inch) pieces (reserve the green parts). Add the white parts to the pan and fry for 5 minutes until soft.

3 Add the stock, bouquet garni and seasoning. Bring to the boil and simmer for 30 minutes or until the chicken is tender.

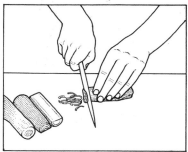

4 Shred the reserved green parts of the leeks, then add to the pan with the prunes. Simmer for a further 30 minutes.

5 To serve, remove the chicken, then cut the meat into large pieces, discarding the skin and bones. Place the meat in a warmed soup tureen, taste and adjust the seasoning of the soup and pour over the meat. Serve hot, garnished with parsley sprigs.

Menu Suggestion
A substantial soup to serve for a hearty lunch with wholemeal bread.

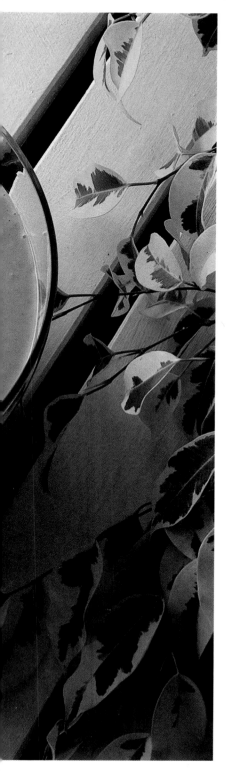

ICED AVOCADO AND CHICKEN SOUP

0.10* £ 293 cals

* plus 2 hours chilling

Serves 6

2 ripe avocados

1 small onion, skinned and chopped

finely grated rind and juice of 1 lemon

142 ml (5 fl oz) natural yogurt

142 ml (5 fl oz) soured cream

600 ml (1 pint) cold chicken stock

175 g (6 oz) cooked chicken, diced

salt and freshly ground pepper

snipped chives, to garnish

1 Halve the avocados and discard the stones. Scoop out the flesh with a teaspoon.

2 Purée together the avocado flesh, onion, lemon rind and juice, yogurt and soured cream in a blender or food processor.

3 Turn out into a large serving bowl or tureen, gradually whisk in the stock, then add the chicken and seasoning to taste. Cover tightly and chill for at least 2 hours.

4 As a garnish, snip chives over the surface of the soup just before serving.

Menu Suggestion

The perfect soup for a summer dinner party or barbecue. Rich and creamy, yet icy cool, serve with crispbreads or wholemeal crackers and chilled white wine.

ICED AVOCADO AND CHICKEN SOUP

Avocado pears are often sold when still hard and unripe. To help them ripen, wrap in newspaper and put in a warm place. After 3–4 days they will be ready. To test for ripeness, apply gentle pressure with your thumb to the tapered end—the skin and flesh should yield slightly.

When choosing avocados, look for the roundish, dark green ones with uneven skins. These often seem to have more flavour than the more egg-shaped, paler green kind with smooth skins.

Avocado flesh discolours quickly on contact with the air, so don't cut open the pears until just before you are ready to make the soup.

CHINESE CHICKEN SOUP

| 1.00 | £ £ ✳ | 260 cals |

Serves 4

25 g (1 oz) dried mushrooms

100 g (4 oz) boneless chicken breast, skinned

1 bunch of spring onions, trimmed

1.1 litres (2 pints) homemade chicken stock (see page 157)

60 ml (4 tbsp) dry or medium sherry

30 ml (2 tbsp) soy sauce, or to taste

5-cm (2-inch) piece of fresh root ginger, peeled and crushed

50 g (2 oz) lean boiled ham

227-g (8-oz) can sliced bamboo shoots, drained

100 g (4 oz) Chinese noodles

salt and freshly ground pepper

prawn crackers, to serve

1 Soak the dried mushrooms in a bowl of warm water for 30 minutes.

2 Meanwhile, cut the chicken into thin matchstick strips and slice the spring onions diagonally into 2.5-cm (1-inch) lengths.

3 Bring the stock to the boil in a large saucepan. Add the sherry, 30 ml (2 tbsp) soy sauce and the ginger, lower the heat then add the chicken, spring onions and drained and sliced mushrooms. Cover and cook for 10 minutes until the chicken is tender.

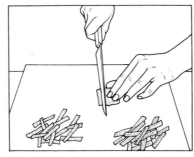

4 Cut the ham and bamboo shoots into thin matchstick strips. Add to the soup with the noodles and simmer for about 5 minutes until the noodles are tender. Add salt and pepper to taste, with more soy sauce if liked. Pour into warmed individual soup bowls and serve immediately, accompanied by prawn crackers.

Menu Suggestion
Serve this ginger-hot soup with crispy prawn crackers as part of a Chinese meal, or with deep-fried spring rolls for an unusual lunch.

CHINESE CHICKEN SOUP
Dried mushrooms, bamboo shoots, fresh ginger and Chinese noodles can all be found in Chinese supermarkets or specialist food shops. Ginger root is also sold in many West Indian and Asian stores. Don't be tempted to substitute fresh mushrooms for dried—the flavour of dried mushrooms is much stronger and helps to give the soup its characteristic body and taste. They are used extensively in Chinese cookery.

CHICKEN WATERZOOI

| 2.00 | £ | ✳* | 205 cals |

* freeze after step 4

Serves 6

| 1.4 kg (3 lb) chicken or boiling fowl, with giblets |
| $\frac{1}{2}$ lemon |
| 2 sticks of celery, chopped |
| 2 leeks, trimmed and chopped |
| 1 medium onion, skinned and chopped |
| 2 carrots, peeled and sliced |
| 1 bouquet garni |
| salt and freshly ground pepper |
| $\frac{1}{2}$ bottle dry white wine |
| 2 egg yolks |
| 90 ml (6 tbsp) single cream |
| 30 ml (2 tbsp) chopped fresh parsley |

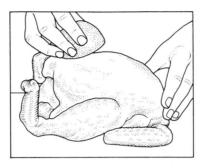

1 Prick the chicken all over with a skewer, then rub with the cut lemon, squeezing the fruit as you do so, to release the juice.

2 Put the chicken in a large saucepan with the giblets, vegetables, bouquet garni and salt and pepper to taste. Pour in the wine, then add enough water to just cover the chicken.

3 Bring the liquid to the boil, then lower the heat and half cover with a lid. Simmer for $1\frac{1}{2}$ hours, or until the meat is tender and beginning to fall away from the bones.

4 Remove the chicken from the liquid. Discard the bouquet garni and the giblets. Cut the chicken flesh into bite-sized pieces, discarding all skin and bones, then return to the liquid.

5 Mix together the egg yolks and cream in a heatproof bowl. Stir in a few ladlefuls of the hot cooking liquid.

6 Return this mixture to the pan. Simmer until thickened, stirring constantly, then add the parsley and taste and adjust seasoning. Serve hot in a warmed soup tureen.

Menu Suggestion
A soup for a special occasion, made substantial with pieces of chicken, vegetables and an egg and cream thickening. Serve with wholemeal bread and chilled dry white wine.

TURKEY AND CHESTNUT SOUP

0.45	✳	156–234 cals

Serves 4–6

25 g (1 oz) butter or margarine

1 large onion, skinned and chopped

225 g (8 oz) Brussels sprouts

900 ml (1½ pints) turkey stock made from leftover carcass (see page 157) and any leftover turkey meat

439-g (15-oz) can whole chestnuts, drained

10 ml (2 tsp) chopped fresh thyme or 5 ml (1 tsp) dried thyme

salt and freshly ground pepper

stock or milk, to finish

sprigs of thyme, to garnish

1 Melt the fat in a large heavy-based saucepan, add the onion and fry gently for 5 minutes until it has softened.

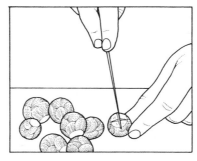

2 Trim the sprouts and cut a cross in the base of each one. Add to the onion, cover the pan with a lid and cook gently for 5 minutes, shaking pan frequently.

3 Pour in the stock and bring to the boil, then add the remaining ingredients, with salt and pepper to taste. Lower the heat, cover and simmer for 30 minutes until the vegetables are tender.

4 Leave to cool slightly, then purée in a blender until smooth. Return to the rinsed-out pan and reheat, then thin down with either stock or milk, according to taste.

5 Taste and adjust seasoning, then pour into warmed individual bowls. Serve hot, garnished with sprigs of thyme.

Menu Suggestion
Serve for an informal family lunch with hot garlic bread, wholemeal toast, cheese on toast or hot sausage rolls.

Starters and Cold Dishes

There's many an occasion
which calls for a meaty
starter, and you'll find
chicken and poultry fit
the bill perfectly: they're
sufficiently light to tempt
the appetite, yet not too
substantial to spoil what's
to follow. This chapter is
full of unusual ideas
using chicken and poultry
in different ways. Simple
and straightforward
starters, elaborate
cold dishes for
sumptuous buffet party
spreads, plus lots of fun
ideas for lunches and
snacks—quick and easy
to follow, yet no less
delicious for that.

MARINATED DUCKLING SALAD

2.00* £ £ 433 cals

*plus 1 hour cooling, 3–4 hours chilling and 30 minutes at room temperature
Serves 6

two 2.3 kg (5 lb) ducklings
salt and freshly ground pepper
10 ml (2 tsp) grated horseradish
finely grated rind and juice of 2 oranges
100 ml (4 fl oz) dry white wine
150 ml (5 fl oz) double cream
90 ml (6 tbsp) thick mayonnaise
orange slices and sprigs of parsley, to garnish

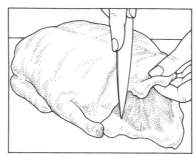

1 Cut away surplus fat from openings, then wipe the ducklings all over with a damp cloth. Pat dry with absorbent kitchen paper. Place side by side on a wire rack over a roasting tin. Prick the birds all over with a sharp skewer and sprinkle generously with salt.

2 Roast in the oven at 180°C (350°F) mark 4 for 1¾ hours or until the birds are really tender. Remove from the oven and leave to cool for 1 hour.

3 Meanwhile, prepare the marinade. Mix together the horseradish, orange rind and juice and white wine, then set aside.

Menu Suggestion
A tangy, yet creamy dish which makes a perfect starter for a dinner party, or an attractive salad for a buffet spread.

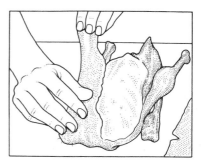

4 While the ducklings are still warm, strip off the crisp breast skin and reserve. Coarsely shred the flesh, discarding all the remaining skin, fat and bones.

5 Toss the duck meat in the marinade, cover and chill for 3–4 hours or overnight.

6 Once chilled, strain off the marinade and pour into a saucepan. Boil rapidly to reduce to 45 ml (3 tbsp). Cool for 5 minutes.

7 Whip the cream lightly and gradually whisk in the marinade until thick, then fold in the mayonnaise. Taste and adjust seasoning, then stir in the duck.

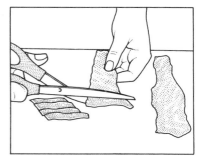

8 Snip the reserved duckling skin into strips and quickly crisp up under a hot grill.

9 To serve, pile the duckling mixture into a serving dish and sprinkle with the duck skin. Leave at room temperature for 30 minutes before serving. Garnish with oranges and sprigs of parsley.

BRANDIED CHICKEN LIVER PÂTÉ

| 0.20* | £ | ✳ | 201–302 cals |

* plus 3–4 hours chilling

Serves 4–6

100 g (4 oz) unsalted butter
225 g (8 oz) chicken livers
30 ml (2 tbsp) brandy
1 garlic clove, skinned
2.5 ml (½ tsp) dried mixed herbs
salt and freshly ground pepper
bay leaves, to garnish

1 Melt half the butter in a heavy frying pan, add the livers and cook them over moderate heat for 5 minutes, stirring so that they cook evenly. The livers should be brown on the outside, and pink, but set, in the centre.

2 Pour the contents of the frying pan straight into a blender or food processor.

3 Pour the brandy into the pan and bring quickly to the boil, stirring well to incorporate any sediment left on the bottom of the pan. Allow to bubble for 1 minute.

4 Add the brandy and juices to the livers with the garlic and dried herbs and blend until smooth. Blend in the remaining butter and salt and pepper to taste.

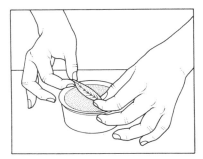

5 Pour the pâté into one terrine, or four to six individual ramekin dishes. Place the bay leaves on top and refrigerate for 3–4 hours before serving.

6 If the pâté is to be kept for several days before serving, pour enough cooled, melted butter over the top to form a complete seal. The pâté will then keep for at least 1 week in the refrigerator.

Menu Suggestion
Serve as a starter with Melba toast or toasted wholemeal or granary bread. A light red or rosé wine would go well with this smooth-textured pâté.

— VARIATION —

A delicious way of varying this rich and flavoursome dish is by substituting 50 g (2 oz) of the chicken livers with the same weight of **sliced mushrooms**. Choose cap or field mushrooms for a more distinctive flavour, and fry them together with the chicken livers in the pan. Instead of using dried mixed herbs, use the same quantity of **dried thyme**, or **5 ml (1 tsp) chopped fresh thyme**.

BANG BANG CHICKEN

2.00* | 252–378 cals

* plus cooling and overnight marinating

Serves 4–6

| 15 ml (1 tbsp) finely chopped fresh root ginger |
| 1.4 kg (3 lb) chicken |
| salt and freshly ground pepper |
| 60 ml (4 tbsp) soy sauce |
| 3 carrots, peeled and very thinly sliced |
| 75 g (3 oz) beansprouts |
| 60 ml (4 tbsp) vegetable oil |
| 30 ml (2 tbsp) sesame oil |
| 30 ml (2 tbsp) sesame seeds |
| 10 ml (2 tsp) crushed dried red chillies |
| 5 ml (1 tsp) soft brown sugar |
| 45 ml (3 tbsp) dry sherry |
| lettuce, to serve |
| spring onion tassels, to garnish |

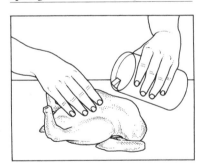

1 Put the ginger inside the cavity of the chicken, then rub the outside of the bird with salt and pepper. Place the bird in a large saucepan and sprinkle over half of the soy sauce. Leave to stand for 30 minutes.

2 Pour enough water into the pan to just cover the chicken. Bring to the boil, then lower the heat, cover and simmer for about 1 hour until the chicken is tender. Leave to cool in the cooking liquid, then remove.

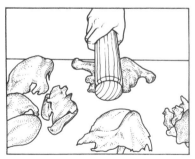

3 Separate the legs and wings from the carcass, then cut the carcass into four. Bang the pieces several times with a rolling pin to loosen the meat from the bones.

4 Cut the meat into neat slices (not too small) or strips. Discard the bones and skin. Combine with carrots and beansprouts.

5 Heat the oils in a heavy-based pan, add the sesame seeds and chillies and fry over brisk heat for a few minutes, stirring until lightly coloured. Remove from the heat and stir in the remaining soy sauce with the sugar and sherry.

6 Pour over the chicken and vegetables, cover and marinate in the refrigerator overnight.

7 To serve, put the chicken and vegetables into a shallow serving dish, lined with lettuce leaves. Pour over any remaining marinade and garnish with spring onion tassels. Serve cold.

Menu Suggestion
A refreshing starter for the first course of a Chinese meal. Serve with a dry white wine.

CRISPY CHICKEN PARCELS

0.45* ⬚ ⬚ £ ✳*

803–857 cals

* plus 30 minutes chilling; freeze after step 5

Serves 4

25 g (1 oz) butter or margarine
50 g (2 oz) flour
300 ml (½ pint) milk
225 g (8 oz) cooked chicken, diced
15 ml (1 tbsp) chopped fresh tarragon or 10 ml (2 tsp) dried tarragon
75 g (3 oz) Gruyère cheese, grated
good pinch of ground mace
salt and freshly ground pepper
15 ml (1 tbsp) vegetable oil
8–12 cannelloni tubes
180 ml (12 tbsp) dried breadcrumbs
180 ml (12 tbsp) grated Parmesan cheese
1 egg, beaten
oil, for deep-frying

1 Melt the fat in a heavy-based saucepan, sprinkle in the flour and cook for 2 minutes, stirring.

2 Remove from the heat and gradually stir in the milk, then bring to the boil, stirring all the time until very thick. Add the chicken, tarragon, Gruyère, mace and salt and pepper to taste. Stir to mix.

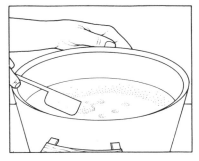

3 Bring a large pan of salted water to the boil, then swirl in the oil. Drop in the cannelloni. Simmer for 5 minutes, drain.

4 Using a teaspoon, or a piping bag fitted with a large plain nozzle, fill each cannelloni tube with the chicken mixture. Pinch the edges to seal.

5 Mix the breadcrumbs and Parmesan in a shallow bowl. Dip the cannelloni tubes first in the beaten egg, then in the breadcrumbs mixed with the Parmesan, making sure they are evenly coated. Chill in the refrigerator for 30 minutes.

6 Heat the oil in a deep-fryer to 180°C (350°F). Deep-fry the parcels a few at a time until golden brown and crisp. Drain on absorbent kitchen paper while frying the remainder. Serve hot.

Menu Suggestion
A substantial, hot starter which needs no accompaniment other than a dry white wine. Can also be served for a tasty lunchtime snack, with a mixed salad.

RAISED CHICKEN AND PHEASANT PIE

3.00* ⬠ £ £ 470 cals

* plus 30 minutes cooling and 2–3 hours chilling

Serves 12

For the pastry

350 g (12 oz) flour

5 ml (1 tsp) salt

75 g (3 oz) butter or block margarine

75 g (3 oz) lard

60 ml (4 tbsp) cold water

1 egg

For the filling

6 eggs

2 medium onions, skinned

1 large garlic clove, skinned

225 g (8 oz) chicken livers

450 g (1 lb) boneless chicken breast, skinned

225 g (8 oz) boneless pheasant meat

275 g (10 oz) streaky bacon, rinded

30 ml (2 tbsp) brandy

7.5 ml (1½ tsp) dried sage or 5 ml (1 tsp) chopped fresh sage

5 ml (1 tsp) salt

freshly ground pepper

1 Make the pastry. Sift the flour and salt into a mound on a clean, dry work surface and make a large well in the centre. Cut up the fats and place them in the well. Add the water and 1 egg.

2 Blend the well ingredients with the fingertips of one hand, until smooth and evenly blended. Work gently at first so that the water and egg don't splash out; and try not to work in the flour at this stage or the pastry may be toughened.

3 With a palette knife, cut the flour through the well ingredients, working them together with the fingertips of your other hand until evenly mixed.

4 Gradually knead the dough together, using your whole hand. Knead until smooth. Wrap the dough in cling film and chill in the refrigerator for 30 minutes.

5 Meanwhile, make the filling. Hard-boil 4 eggs, cool, then shell and put to one side. Mince the onions and garlic into a large bowl together with the chicken livers, chicken and pheasant meat and 100 g (4 oz) of the streaky bacon. Add the brandy, sage, 1 egg, the salt and plenty of pepper; mix thoroughly.

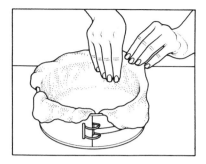

7 Stretch out the remaining bacon rashers with a blunt-edged knife. Lay them across the pastry base and up the sides. Fill with half the minced mixture and press the hard-boiled eggs gently down into it to form a circle. Spread the remaining minced mixture over the eggs to cover completely. Fold any ends of bacon rashers across the top of the filling.

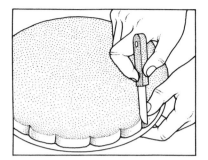

6 Roll out three quarters of the pastry to a 33-cm (13-inch) round on a lightly floured work surface. Lift into a 20.5-cm (8-inch) spring-form tin. Press the dough into the corners and bring it up the sides.

8 Roll out the rest of the pastry to a 23-cm (9-inch) round and top the pie, reserving the trimmings. Knock the pastry edges together to form a good seal and flute the edges. To do this, press pastry edge outwards with the thumb while pulling gently inwards with a blunt knife.

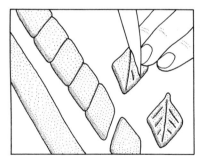

9 Roll out pastry trimmings to an oblong and cut into diamond shapes. Mark 'vein' lines on these 'leaves', twist them and put on top of the pie. Make a small central hole. Glaze with a lightly beaten egg. Chill for 30 minutes.

10 Bake on a baking sheet in the oven at 180°C (350°F) mark 4 for $1\frac{3}{4}$ hours, covering with foil when starting to brown.

11 Leave in the tin for 30 minutes, then remove tin and refrigerate for 2–3 hours.

Menu Suggestion
A sumptuously rich pie for a cold buffet spread. Serve with a red wine, salads and pickles.

SPINACH AND CHICKEN TERRINE

| 1.55 | £ £ | 260 cals |

Serves 8

450 g (1 lb) boneless chicken breast, skinned

200 ml (7 fl oz) double cream

300 ml (½ pint) milk

3 eggs

1 garlic clove, skinned and crushed

salt and freshly ground pepper

900 g (2 lb) fresh spinach, washed

1 Grease a 1.4-litre (2½-pint) loaf tin. In a blender or food processor, purée together the chicken, cream, milk and eggs until very smooth. Stir in the crushed garlic and season well.

2 Blanch enough spinach leaves to line the prepared loaf tin, by plunging in boiling water until tender, drain.

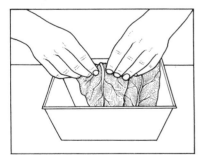

3 Line the base and sides of the prepared loaf tin with the blanched spinach leaves.

4 Put the remaining spinach in a saucepan with salt (but no extra liquid) and cook for 5–7 minutes, until just tender; drain and finely chop.

5 Spoon half the chicken mixture into the lined tin. Carefully place the chopped spinach in a layer over the chicken. Finish with the remaining chicken mixture.

6 Cover with greased foil. Place in a roasting tin half filled with boiling water and cook in the oven at 170°C (325°F) mark 3 for about 1 hour 20 minutes until firm.

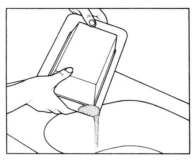

7 Invert the loaf tin on to a flat serving plate. With the tin still in place, pour off any excess liquid. Remove tin and serve the terrine hot or cold, sliced.

Menu Suggestion

A layered terrine which makes a sensational dinner party starter served hot, or an attractive addition to a buffet party spread served cold.

SPINACH AND CHICKEN TERRINE

When cooking spinach for any dish it is important to drain it thoroughly. It's always surprising just how much liquid there is in cooked spinach—even when no water has been added to the pan during cooking. To drain it thoroughly, place the cooked spinach in a colander and press down firmly, using a plate or large saucer. Slice the spinach roughly while still in the colander and press down again before turning onto a board to chop finely.

CHICKEN TIKKA

| 0.40* | 136 cals |

* plus 24 hours marinating

Serves 4

4 boneless chicken breasts, skinned and cut into even-sized cubes

juice of 1 lemon

about 5 ml (1 tsp) salt

few drops each of red and yellow food colouring

2 small onions, skinned and cut into wedges

1 large green pepper, cored, seeded and cut into large chunks

lemon wedges, lettuce leaves and onion rings, to serve

For the marinade

142 ml (5 oz) natural yogurt

2.5-cm (1-inch) piece of fresh root ginger, peeled and crushed

2 garlic cloves, skinned and crushed

15 ml (1 tbsp) white wine vinegar

10 ml (2 tsp) garam masala

5 ml (1 tsp) chilli powder

1 Put the cubes of chicken in a bowl and sprinkle them with the lemon juice and the salt. Stir well and set aside.

2 Make the marinade. Put the yogurt in a blender or food processor with the ginger, garlic, vinegar, garam masala and chilli powder. Work until everything is well combined.

3 Mix the food colouring into the chicken until it turns a bright orange colour. Add the yogurt marinade and stir well to mix, then cover and leave to marinate in the refrigerator for 24 hours. Turn the chicken in the marinade from time to time.

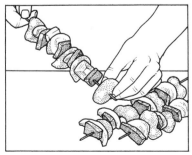

4 Thread the chicken pieces on to oiled kebab skewers, alternating with onion and pepper.

5 Cook the tikka under a preheated hot grill (or preferably on a barbecue) for about 15 minutes until tender. Turn the skewers frequently during cooking. Serve hot, with lemon wedges, lettuce and onion rings.

Menu Suggestion
Serve as a first course to an Indian meal or as part of a barbecue party with poppadoms or warm Indian bread such as naan, chapati or paratha. Mango chutney, lime pickle and yogurt and cucumber salad (raita) also go well with Chicken Tikka. Serve ice-cold lager to drink.

CHICKEN AND GRAPE SALAD

| 1.40* | 🝙 £ £ | 275–413 cals |

* plus 2 hours cooling

Serves 4

| 1.4 kg (3 lb) chicken |
| 1 medium onion, skinned |
| 1 carrot, peeled |
| 1 bay leaf |
| 6 peppercorns |
| 2 eggs |
| 90 ml (6 tbsp) lemon juice |
| 45 ml (3 tbsp) clear honey |
| 150 ml (5 fl oz) whipping cream |
| 225 g (8 oz) green grapes |
| 50 g (2 oz) raisins |
| salt and freshly ground pepper |
| lettuce, to serve |

1 Put the chicken in a large saucepan with the onion, carrot, bay leaf and peppercorns. Pour in enough water to just cover, and poach for about 1 hour, until tender. Cool for at least 2 hours in the stock, then remove and cut the flesh into bite-size pieces, discarding skin and bones.

2 Beat the eggs with 60 ml (4 tbsp) lemon juice and the honey. Put in a double boiler or in a basin standing over a saucepan of hot water and cook, stirring, until thick. Remove from the heat, cover with damp greaseproof paper and cool for 45 minutes.

3 Whip the cream until it is thick, then gently fold it into the cold lemon mixture.

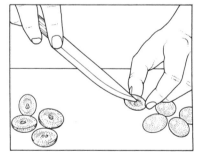

4 Halve the grapes, then flick out the seeds with the point of a sharp knife. Add grapes to the chicken with remaining lemon juice, the raisins and sauce. Season.

5 Pile the salad into a lettuce-lined serving dish. Serve at room temperature.

Menu Suggestion
A subtly-flavoured, light salad — perfect for a summer lunch outside. Serve with fresh French bread or a rice salad.

CLUB SANDWICHES

| 0.10 | 595 cals |

Serves 2

6 rashers streaky bacon, rinded
6 slices white bread, toasted
about 45 ml (3 tbsp) mayonnaise
a few lettuce leaves
2 large slices cooked turkey
salt and freshly ground pepper
1 large tomato, sliced

1 Fry the bacon in its own fat until crisp; drain on absorbent kitchen paper. Spread one side of each slice of toast with some of the mayonnaise.

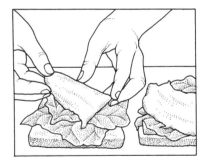

2 Arrange half the lettuce on two slices of toast; top with turkey. Sprinkle with salt and pepper then add another slice of toast, mayonnaise side up.

3 Arrange the rest of the lettuce, the tomato slices, and the bacon on the two sandwiches. Top with the remaining toast slices, mayonnaise side down.

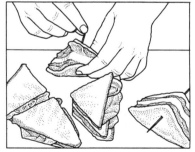

4 Cut the sandwiches diagonally into quarters and secure each one with a cocktail stick. Arrange, crust sides down, on two plates.

Menu Suggestion
A hearty American-style snack for any time of day. Serve with ice-cold lager or beer.

CHAUDFROID OF CHICKEN

`1.45*` 🍴 🍴 `143 cals`

* plus 3 hours cooling and 1 hour chilling

Serves 4

4 boneless chicken breasts

1 bay leaf

1 carrot, peeled and roughly chopped

1 medium onion, skinned and quartered

1 bouquet garni

25 g (1 oz) aspic powder

300 ml (½ pint) béchamel sauce (see page 158)

strips of cucumber skin, slices of radish, mustard and cress leaves, and strips of lemon rind, to garnish as desired

1 Put the chicken portions in a large saucepan with enough cold water to cover. Add the bay leaf, carrot, onion and bouquet garni. Slowly bring to the boil, cover and simmer for 35–40 minutes until tender. Carefully lift the chicken out of the stock and drain. Leave chicken for about 3 hours until completely cool.

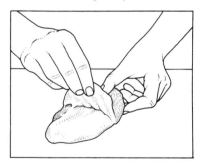

2 Carefully skin the cold chicken breasts and stand on a cooling rack over a tray or large plate.

3 Make up the aspic to 600 ml (1 pint) as directed on the packet. For chopped aspic garnish, pour 300 ml (½ pint) of the aspic into a shallow tin and refrigerate for 30 minutes. Leave the remaining aspic until it has almost reached setting point. Add 150 ml (¼ pint) of the aspic to the béchamel sauce, stir in lightly and allow it to thicken but not set. Keep the remaining aspic in a basin standing in a bowl of lukewarm water.

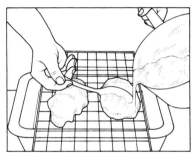

4 Coat the chicken pieces by spooning the sauce steadily over them to give a smooth, even surface. Allow the excess to run off and collect in the tray. Leave to set for 15 minutes in the refrigerator.

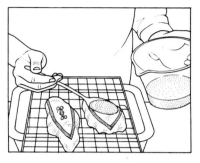

5 Garnish the chicken simply with the chosen garnish, then carefully spoon over the remaining aspic (which should be at setting point), so that the coated pieces are completely covered but the garnish is not disturbed. Leave to set for about 15–20 minutes before transferring to a serving dish.

6 Turn out the set aspic on to damp greaseproof paper, chop roughly with a wet knife and spoon carefully around the chicken. Chill for about 30 minutes before serving.

Menu Suggestion
A stunning table centrepiece for a special buffet party. Serve with a selection of salads—and champagne!

CHAUDFROID OF CHICKEN

The history of this dish goes back a long way. Some say it dates from 1759 when it was invented in the kitchens of a French nobleman who, being delayed from attending his own banquet, was served a dish of fricassée of chicken long after his guests had finished eating. Instead of being hot, the chicken had turned cold, but the nobleman enjoyed his meal so much that he requested the same dish to be served again at a future date.

There is another theory that the dish dates as far back as Roman times—this idea is based on discoveries at excavations in Pompeii, but this has never been proved. What is certain, though, is that chaudfroid of chicken has firmly taken its place in the classic style of French cuisine. Traditionally, not just chicken, but any fowl or game was served in this way. The finished dish would be elaborately presented at the table, usually arranged pyramid-style on a decorated base and garnished with slivers of truffle and other prepared foods, all enclosed in a shiny aspic glaze.

CHICKEN WITH CURRIED LEMON MAYONNAISE

| 1.30* | 871 cals |

* plus about $2\frac{1}{4}$ hours cooling and 30 minutes chilling

Serves 4

1.4 kg (3 lb) chicken

150 ml ($\frac{1}{4}$ pint) dry white wine

1 strip of lemon rind

1 bouquet garni

6 black peppercorns

salt and freshly ground pepper

15 g ($\frac{1}{2}$ oz) butter or margarine

1 small onion, skinned and chopped

15 ml (1 tbsp) curry powder

2 sticks of celery, finely chopped

175 ml (6 fl oz) thick mayonnaise

30 ml (2 tbsp) apricot jam

finely grated rind and juice of 1 lemon

1 red or green pepper, cored, seeded and diced

2 red-skinned eating apples

150 ml (5 fl oz) double or whipping cream

lettuce, to serve

1 Put the chicken in a deep saucepan with the wine, enough water to just cover the bird, lemon rind, bouquet garni, peppercorns and a good pinch of salt. Cover and simmer for $1-1\frac{1}{4}$ hours until the chicken is tender, then leave for about 2 hours to cool in the liquid.

2 Remove the chicken from the liquid; strain the liquid into a saucepan, then boil until reduced to a few tablespoons. Cool for 5 minutes.

3 Meanwhile, remove the chicken from the bones, and dice the meat, discarding all skin.

4 Melt the fat in a small pan, add the onion and curry powder and fry until soft. Add celery and fry for 2 minutes, stirring. Cool for 10 minutes.

5 Add the onion and celery to the mayonnaise with the apricot jam, lemon rind and juice and the diced pepper. Thin with the reduced cooking liquid. Taste and adjust seasoning.

6 Core and dice or slice the apples, but do not peel them. Whip the cream until thick, then fold into the mayonnaise with the apples and chicken. Pile into a salad bowl lined with lettuce leaves. Chill for about 30 minutes before serving.

Menu Suggestion
Serve for a summer lunch with poppadoms or pitta bread and chilled lager or dry white wine.

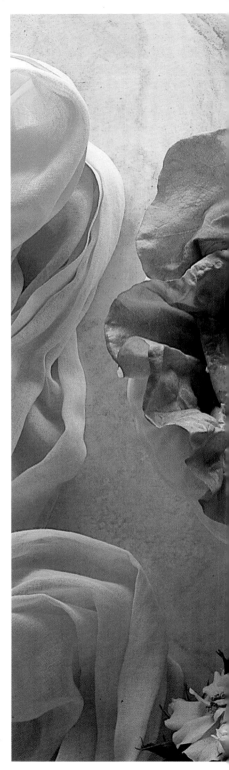

PICNIC LOAF

2.00* ✳ 205 cals

* plus 3–4 hours cooling

Serves 8

125 g (4 oz) streaky bacon

125 g (4 oz) chicken livers, finely
 chopped

1 medium onion, skinned and
 finely chopped

350 g (12 oz) boneless chicken
 breast, skinned and minced

75 g (3 oz) fresh wholemeal
 breadcrumbs

30 ml (2 tbsp) Worcestershire sauce

salt and freshly ground pepper

2 eggs, beaten

60 ml (4 tbsp) cranberry sauce

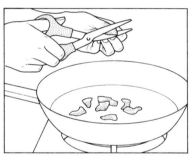

1 Cut the rind off the bacon and
 snip the flesh into small pieces
directly into a frying pan.

2 Fry the bacon until the fat
 runs, then add the finely
chopped chicken livers and onion.
Fry, stirring constantly, for 2–3
minutes, then leave to cool.

3 In a bowl or food processor,
 pound together the chicken
and breadcrumbs. Add the cool
liver mixture, the Worcestershire
sauce and salt and pepper to taste
and mix well. Bind with the eggs.

4 Base line a 750-ml (1¼-pint)
 shallow loaf tin. Spoon in the
cranberry sauce. Spoon the
chicken mixture on top. Cover
with a piece of greased foil.

5 Place in a roasting tin half
 filled with boiling water and
cook in the oven at 180°C (350°F)
mark 4 for about 1½ hours until
firm. Cool for 1 hour in the tin
then refrigerate for 2–3 hours
before turning out.

Menu Suggestion

Moist and tasty Picnic Loaf is
ideal for carrying on picnics. Cut
up and wrap individual slices in
cling film or foil before leaving
home, then serve with potato and
mixed salads, chutney and pickle,
and extra cranberry sauce if liked.

PICNIC LOAF

The wholemeal breadcrumbs
used here make a tasty change
from the usual white ones, which
really have very little flavour of
their own.

 To make the breadcrumbs,
choose day-old bread, as it will
crumb more easily than very
fresh bread which is too moist to
work with easily. Thickly slice
the bread then cut off the crusts
with a sharp knife. Grate the
bread on the coarse side of a
grater. Alternatively, break it
into pieces and turn into crumbs
in a liquidiser or food processor.

PANCAKE ROLLS

| 0.40 | 🔲 🔲 £ ✳* | 99 cals |

* freeze after step 7

Makes 8

225 g (8 oz) cooked chicken

15 ml (1 tbsp) sesame or vegetable oil

1 small bunch of spring onions, trimmed and finely chopped

3 garlic cloves, skinned and crushed

2.5-cm (1-inch) piece of fresh root ginger, peeled and crushed

100 g (4 oz) beansprouts

2 carrots, peeled and grated

15 ml (1 tbsp) soy sauce

2.5 ml ($\frac{1}{2}$ tsp) soft brown sugar

salt and freshly ground pepper

8 squares of spring roll pastry, defrosted if frozen

vegetable oil, for deep-frying

1 Cut the chicken into thin strips, discarding any pieces of skin or bone. Set aside.

2 Heat the 15 ml (1 tbsp) oil in a wok or frying pan, add the spring onions, garlic and ginger and fry gently for 5 minutes until soft. Add the beansprouts and carrot and fry for a further 2 minutes, stirring constantly.

3 Turn the vegetables into a bowl, add the chicken, and mix with the soy sauce, sugar and salt and pepper to taste.

4 Divide the filling mixture equally into eight, then form each portion into a roll shape.

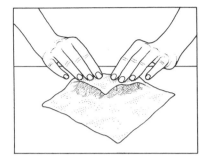

5 Place one roll on one sheet of pastry, over the corner nearest to you. Fold over the corner.

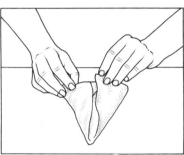

6 Fold in the corner at right angles to the first corner, then fold in the opposite corner.

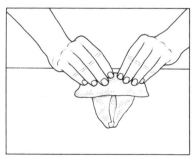

7 Roll up the filling in the pastry until the last corner is reached, so that the filling is completely enclosed. Seal with a little water.

8 Heat the oil to 180°C (350°F), then deep-fry the rolls for about 5 minutes. Drain well.

Menu Suggestion

Serve as a first course.

CHICKEN AND AVOCADO MOUSSE

0.30* ☐ £ £ ✳* 411 cals

* plus 4 hours setting time; freeze for 1
month only or avocado may discolour

Serves 8

**300 ml (½ pint) homemade chicken
stock (see page 157)**

15 ml (3 tsp) gelatine

2 ripe avocados

juice of ½ a lemon

**225 g (8 oz) cooked chicken, minced
or very finely diced**

**1 bunch of spring onions, trimmed
and very finely chopped**

5 ml (1 tsp) Worcestershire sauce

pinch of cayenne pepper

salt

150 ml (5 fl oz) double cream

150 ml (¼ pint) thick mayonnaise

avocado slices, to garnish

1 Place the stock in a bowl and
sprinkle in the gelatine. Stand
the bowl over a saucepan of hot
water and heat gently until dis-
solved. Leave to cool.

2 Halve, stone and peel the
avocados. Mash the flesh with
the lemon juice (to prevent the
avocados discolouring).

3 Fold the chicken into the avocados with the spring onions,
Worcestershire sauce, cayenne
pepper and salt to taste. Stir in the
cooled gelatine.

4 Whip the cream until thick,
then fold into the chicken and
avocado mixture with the mayonnaise. Taste and adjust seasoning.

5 Turn the mixture into a lightly
oiled 900-ml (1½-pint) mould,
cover and refrigerate for 4 hours
until set.

6 Unmould and serve im-
mediately (to prevent the
avocado discolouring), with
avocado slices to garnish.

Menu Suggestion

A luxurious dinner party starter.
Serve with Melba toast and a
chilled dry white wine.

Smoked Chicken and Orange Appetiser

0.50*	772 cals

* plus 30 minutes chilling

Serves 4

900 g (2 lb) smoked chicken

4 oranges

135 ml (9 tbsp) sunflower or vegetable oil

juice of 1 orange

1.25 ml ($\frac{1}{4}$ tsp) ground allspice or mixed spice

pinch of sugar

salt and freshly ground pepper

sprigs of curly endive, to garnish

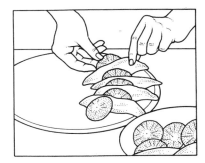

1 Remove all the meat from the chicken carcass, cutting the slices thinly and evenly.

2 Remove the skin and pith from the oranges with a sharp, serrated knife, working in a spiral and using a sawing action.

3 Carefully cut the prepared orange crossways into thin, even rounds.

4 Arrange the chicken and orange slices in a fan shape on four individual serving plates.

5 Make the dressing. Put the oil, orange juice, spice and sugar in a screw-top jar with salt and pepper to taste. Shake vigorously to combine, then taste and adjust spice and seasoning.

6 Pour the dressing over the salad, then refrigerate for at least 30 minutes so that the flavours are absorbed. Garnish each plate with a sprig or two of endive just before serving.

Menu Suggestion

A dinner party starter or buffet party salad with a difference—the combination of smoky-flavoured chicken and sweet oranges is most unusual, yet quite delicious. Serve with fresh French bread and butter, and chilled dry white wine.

SMOKED CHICKEN AND ORANGE APPETISER

Chicken is either cured by a hot-smoking process, or it is cooked and then smoked. Other poultry and game such as turkey, guinea fowl and quail are treated in the same way. The flesh of smoked chicken is tender and juicy with a flavour similar to ham. Once purchased, smoked chicken has the same keeping qualities as fresh chicken and should be treated accordingly.

LEMON AND ALMOND LIVER PÂTÉ

0.25*	£ £	✻	446–595 cals

* plus overnight chilling

Serves 6–8

450 g (1 lb) turkey or chicken livers

225 g (8 oz) butter, softened

2 medium onions, skinned and sliced

10 ml (2 tsp) prepared mustard

15 ml (1 tbsp) lemon juice

finely grated rind of 1 lemon

30 ml (2 tbsp) double cream

5 ml (1 tsp) grated nutmeg

30 ml (2 tbsp) brandy

175 g (6 oz) ground almonds

salt and freshly ground pepper

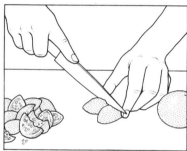

1 Trim the livers. Melt 50 g (2 oz) butter in a frying pan and fry the onion gently for 5 minutes until soft. Add the livers to the pan and cook gently for a further 5 minutes.

2 Purée the contents of the pan in a blender or food processor. Then leave for 10 minutes to cool slightly.

3 Beat in 50 g (2 oz) butter and the rest of the ingredients except the remaining butter. Season well, then spoon into six to eight individual ramekin dishes.

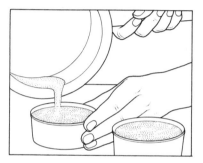

4 Melt the remaining butter and pour over the tops of the pâtés. Chill overnight before using.

Menu Suggestion
A delicate pâté to serve for a special dinner party starter with Melba toast and a well-chilled dry white wine.

LEMON AND ALMOND LIVER PÂTÉ

The unusual addition of almonds adds an exotic touch to this liver pâté. Although almonds are available ready ground, you can also buy them in and out of their shells, blanched, flaked, shredded and diced. You can make your own ground almonds by simply putting any of these prepared, shelled almonds into a coffee grinder and switching the motor on and off a couple of times, when they will be reduced to a fine powder ready for use.

DUCK AND ORANGE TERRINE

| 3.30* | 🍴 | £ £ | 133–166 cals |

* plus 2 hours cooling, 2¼ hours chilling and 30 minutes at room temperature

Serves 8–10

1.8 kg (4 lb) duckling

350 g (12 oz) pork belly, skin removed

125 g (4 oz) lamb's liver

1 medium onion, skinned

1 orange

1 garlic clove, skinned and crushed

salt and freshly ground pepper

2.5 ml (½ tsp) ground mace

15 ml (1 tbsp) chopped fresh parsley

30 ml (2 tbsp) sherry

15 g (½ oz) aspic powder, orange slices and celery leaves, to garnish

1 Completely remove the skin and layer of fat from the duckling and discard.

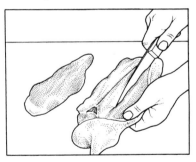

2 Cut the breast portion away from the bird. Remove the rest of the flesh—about 350 g (12 oz).

3 Finely mince the duckling flesh (except the breast) in a blender or food processor with the pork, liver and onion. Grate the rind of the orange.

4 Segment the flesh of the orange, free of membrane, over a bowl to collect any juice. Cut segments into small pieces.

5 In a bowl, combine the minced meats, orange segments and juice with all the remaining ingredients, except the breast meat and garnish.

6 Press half the mixture into a 1.1-litre (2-pint) terrine. Lay the breast portions on top, then cover with the remaining mixture, pressing it down well. Cover with foil and lid.

7 Place the terrine in a roasting tin half filled with boiling water. Cook in the oven at 170°C (325°F) mark 3 for 3 hours until firm. Remove from the roasting tin, weight down and leave for 2 hours until cold, then refrigerate for about 2 hours. Scrape off any solidified fat. Drain away juices.

8 Make up the aspic to 300 ml (½ pint) as directed on the packet. Garnish the terrine with orange slices and celery leaves. Spoon aspic over when nearly set. Refrigerate for 15–20 minutes. Leave at room temperature for 30 minutes before serving.

Menu Suggestion

A rich, strongly-flavoured terrine, ideal for a winter dinner party or festive buffet. Serve with a crisp green salad, tossed in a sharp vinaigrette dressing, and French bread. A rosé or light red wine would be the most suitable drink.

Everyday Dishes

Chicken and poultry are just right for everyday meals. With hardly any waste compared with other meats, they're so economical. Quick to cook, they're also perfect for last-minute meals when the family's hungry and there's very little time to rustle up a meal. It's all nutritious, protein-packed meat too, which everyone enjoys most of all.

TURKEY FRICASSÉE

| 0.25 | ✳* | 471 cals |

* freeze without the cream

Serves 4

175 g (6 oz) button mushrooms

65 g (2½ oz) butter or margarine

50 g (2 oz) flour

600 ml (1 pint) chicken or turkey stock (see page 157)

15 ml (1 tbsp) lemon juice

700 g (1½ lb) cooked turkey, cut into bite-size pieces

salt and freshly ground pepper

45 ml (3 tbsp) double cream

lemon slices dipped in chopped fresh parsley, to garnish

1 Wipe the mushrooms, then slice thinly. Melt 15 g (½ oz) fat in a frying pan and sauté the mushrooms for 5 minutes until they are soft.

2 Melt the remaining fat in a saucepan. Add the flour and cook, stirring, for 2 minutes. Remove from the heat and gradually stir in the stock. Bring to the boil and cook for about 5 minutes, stirring until the sauce thickens.

3 Add the lemon juice to the sauce with the turkey, mushrooms and seasoning. Heat gently, then stir in the cream. Serve hot, garnished with the lemon slices.

Menu Suggestion

This rich fricassée of turkey and mushrooms in a creamy sauce is best served with plain boiled white rice and a mixed salad, or a colourful vegetable such as buttered carrots tossed in chopped fresh herbs.

CHICKEN PAPRIKASH

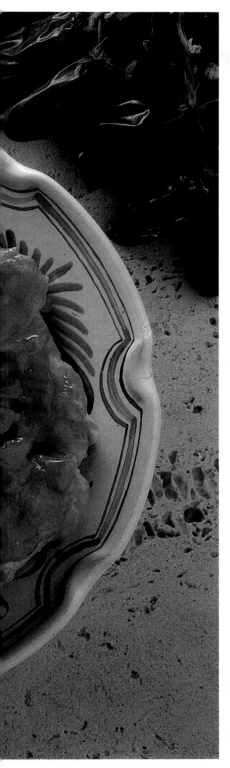

| 1.30 | ✳* | 398 cals |

* freeze after step 5

Serves 4

1.4 kg (3 lb) chicken, jointed into 8
   pieces (see page 151)

50 g (2 oz) flour

salt and freshly ground pepper

50 g (2 oz) butter or chicken fat

450 g (1 lb) onions, skinned and
   sliced

1 red pepper, cored, seeded and
   sliced

15 ml (1 tbsp) paprika

1 garlic clove, skinned and crushed

397-g (14-oz) can tomatoes

300 ml (½ pint) chicken stock

1 bay leaf

142 ml (5 fl oz) soured cream

1 Toss the chicken joints in the
flour, liberally seasoned with
salt and pepper, to coat.

2 Melt the fat in a frying pan
and fry the chicken joints until
golden brown. Transfer the joints
to a casserole large enough to take
them in a single layer.

3 Add the onions and red pepper
to the frying pan and fry
gently for 5 minutes until soft. Stir
in the paprika, garlic and any remaining flour. Cook gently, stirring, for a few minutes.

4 Add the tomatoes with their
juice, the stock and bay leaf.
Season and bring to the boil. Pour
over the chicken.

5 Cover tightly and cook in the
oven at 170°C (325°F) mark 3
for about 1 hour until the chicken
is tender. Discard the bay leaf.

6 Stir half the soured cream into
the casserole. Spoon the remaining soured cream over the top
and serve immediately.

Menu Suggestion
This main course chicken dish,
with its rich and pungent sauce,
needs plain accompaniments such
as jacket baked potatoes or boiled
rice, and a green salad tossed in
vinaigrette dressing.

CHICKEN PAPRIKASH

There often seems to be some
confusion over the difference
between paprika, which is used
in this dish, and cayenne pepper.
The reason for this is probably
because in the dried powdered
form they look very similar, but
in fact, they are derived from
different sources.

Cayenne pepper is made from
ground dried chillies (from
which Tabasco sauce is also
made), and it has a pungent, hot
flavour. Paprika is made from
sweet red peppers. Probably the
best type to choose is the mild
Hungarian paprika, sometimes
described as sweet paprika.

SESAME OVEN-FRIED DRUMSTICKS

| 0.50* | ✳* | 350 cals |

* plus 1 hour marinating; freeze after step 3

Serves 4

8 even-sized chicken drumsticks, skinned

45 ml (3 tbsp) lemon juice

50 g (2 oz) flour

salt and freshly ground pepper

1 egg, beaten

about 125 g (4 oz) sesame seeds

finely grated rind of $\frac{1}{2}$ a lemon

125 g (4 oz) butter, melted

lemon wedges and green salad, to serve

1 Prick the skinned drumsticks all over with a fork. Place in a shallow dish with the lemon juice and marinate for 1 hour, turning from time to time.

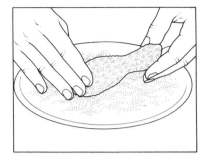

2 Remove the drumsticks from the marinade, coat in the flour seasoned with salt and pepper, then in beaten egg.

3 Mix together the sesame seeds and grated lemon rind, then use to coat the drumsticks.

4 Put into a roasting tin with the melted butter and marinade juices and cook in the oven at 190°C (375°F) mark 5 for 40–45 minutes, until tender, basting frequently. Serve hot, with lemon wedges and a green salad.

Menu Suggestion
Serve these crisp and crunchy chicken drumsticks with a mixed salad for a light lunch, or with a salad such as coleslaw and French fries for a more substantial evening meal.

SPANISH CHICKEN AND RICE

| 1.30 | ✳ | 654 cals |

Serves 4

1.4 kg (3 lb) chicken, jointed into 8 pieces (see page 151)

30 ml (2 tbsp) flour

salt and freshly ground pepper

60 ml (4 tbsp) vegetable oil

1 medium onion, skinned and chopped

396-g (14-oz) can tomatoes

170-g (6-oz) can pimientoes, drained and sliced

2 chicken stock cubes, crumbled

8 stuffed olives

175 g (6 oz) long grain rice

225 g (8 oz) chorizo sausages, cut into 1-cm (½-inch) slices

100 g (4 oz) frozen peas

watercress sprigs, to garnish

1 Toss the chicken joints in the flour seasoned with salt and pepper. Heat the oil in a large saucepan, brown the chicken on all sides and remove. Add the onion and fry until golden brown.

2 Drain the tomatoes and add enough water to make the juice up to 450 ml (¾ pint).

3 Return the chicken to the pan. Add the tomato juice, the tomatoes and the next five ingredients. Season to taste.

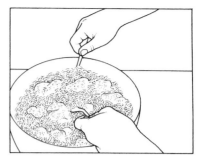

4 Cover the pan tightly and simmer gently for 45 minutes, forking carefully through the rice occasionally to prevent it sticking.

5 Add the peas to the pan, cover again and simmer for a further 30 minutes until the chicken is tender. Before serving, taste and adjust seasoning and garnish with the sprigs of watercress.

Menu Suggestion
A substantial main course dish needing no further accompaniment.

CHICKEN EGGAH

| 1.40 | 246–369 cals |

Serves 4–6

2 chicken portions

600 ml (1 pint) homemade chicken stock (see page 157)

10 ml (2 tsp) ground cumin

1.25 ml ($\frac{1}{4}$ tsp) chilli powder

salt and freshly ground pepper

1.1 litres (2 pints) water

100 g (4 oz) Chinese egg noodles

6 eggs

50 g (2 oz) butter or margarine

1 medium onion, skinned and sliced

1 garlic clove, skinned and crushed

10 ml (2 tsp) paprika

1 Put the chicken portions in a large saucepan, then add the chicken stock, cumin and chilli powder, with salt and pepper to taste. Simmer for 30 minutes or until the chicken is tender.

2 Remove the chicken from the pan and set aside. Add the water to the pan and bring to the boil. Add the noodles and boil for about 5 minutes until tender or according to packet instructions. Leave to drain thoroughly in a colander or sieve.

3 Remove the chicken flesh from the bones and discard the skin. Cut the meat into small strips.

4 Use kitchen scissors to cut the cooked, drained egg noodles into short lengths.

5 Beat the eggs lightly in a large bowl, then add the noodles and chicken and stir gently to mix. Melt the fat in a large heavy-based frying pan, add the onion, garlic and paprika and fry gently until soft.

6 Pour in the egg mixture and stir lightly with a fork. Cook over moderate heat for 15 minutes until golden brown underneath.

7 Turn the eggah out on to a plate then slide back into the pan so that the underside is uppermost. Cook for a further 15 minutes until golden brown underneath. Serve hot.

Menu Suggestion
A light lunch or supper dish, this Persian-style omelette can be served with a mixed salad and warm pitta bread.

CHICKEN EGGAH
'Eggah' is an egg-based dish which comes from Middle Eastern countries. It is basically rather like a solid omelette, not intended to be light like the French omelette. An eggah is often quite plain, using eggs and perhaps one or two vegetables; this one is made into more of a meal with the addition of tender strips of chicken and egg noodles, lightly spiced with cumin, chilli and paprika.

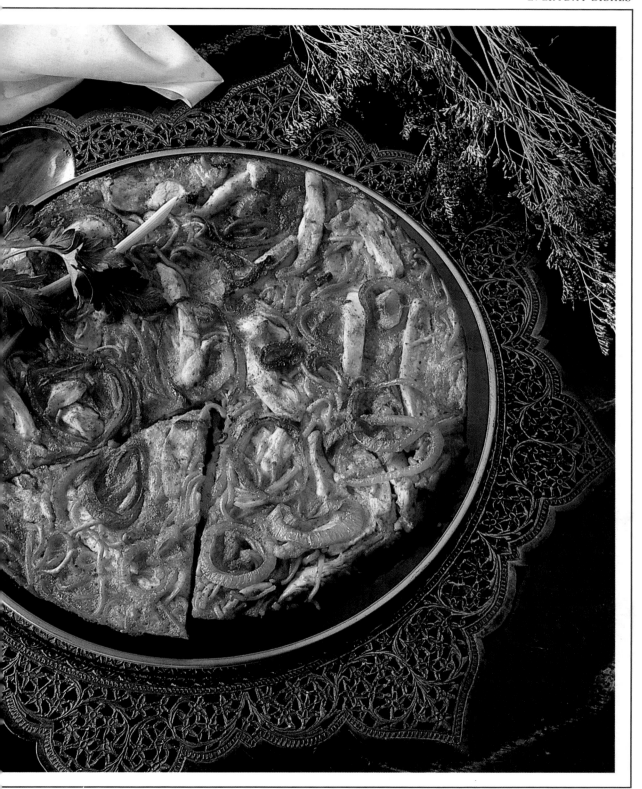

CHICKEN TACOS

| 0.15 | 🍴 | 297 cals |

Serves 6

6 Mexican taco shells
25 g (1 oz) butter or margarine
1 medium onion, skinned and
    chopped
450 g (1 lb) cooked chicken, diced
4 tomatoes, skinned and chopped
salt and freshly ground pepper
shredded lettuce
100 g (4 oz) Cheddar cheese, grated
Tabasco sauce

1   Put the taco shells in the oven to warm according to the instructions on the packet.

2   Make the filling. Melt the fat in a frying pan and fry the onion until soft but not coloured. Stir in the chicken, half the tomatoes and seasoning and heat through.

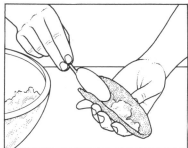

3   Spoon 15–30 ml (1–2 tbsp) filling into each shell. Add a little lettuce, the remaining tomatoes and the cheese with a few drops of Tabasco sauce; serve the filled tacos immediately.

Menu Suggestion
Serve spicy hot tacos as a snack to be eaten with the fingers. Ice-cold lager is the only accompaniment needed, and maybe some fresh fruit such as pineapple to refresh the palate afterwards.

CHICKEN PUFF PIE

| 2.15* | ✳* | 409–613 cals |

* plus about 30 minutes cooling;
freeze after step 8

Serves 4–6

900 g (2 lb) chicken

1 bay leaf

**2 sprigs of fresh rosemary or
marjoram, or 10 ml (2 tsp) dried**

salt and freshly ground pepper

**4 leeks, trimmed, washed and cut
into 2-cm (¾-inch) lengths**

**2 large carrots, peeled and thickly
sliced**

**100 g (4 oz) boiled ham, cut into
bite-size pieces**

25 g (1 oz) butter or margarine

**1 medium onion, skinned and
chopped**

45 ml (3 tbsp) flour

150 ml (¼ pint) milk

60 ml (4 tbsp) double cream

**225 g (8 oz) frozen puff pastry,
defrosted**

1 egg, beaten, to glaze

1 Put the chicken in a large
saucepan with the herbs and
salt and pepper to taste. Cover
with water and bring to the boil,
then cover with a lid and simmer
for 45–60 minutes until the
chicken is tender.

2 Remove the chicken from the
liquid and leave to cool
slightly. Meanwhile, add the leeks
and carrots to the liquid, bring to
the boil and simmer for about 7
minutes until tender but still
crunchy. Remove from the pan
with a slotted spoon.

3 Remove the chicken meat
from the bones, discarding the
skin. Cut into bite-size chunks.

4 Mix the chicken with the ham
and cooked leeks and carrots in
a 1.1-litre (2-pint) pie dish.

5 Melt the fat in a clean saucepan, add the onion and fry
gently until soft. Sprinkle in the
flour and cook for 1–2 minutes,
stirring, then gradually add 600 ml
(1 pint) of the cooking liquid (discarding the bay leaf and herb
sprigs, if used). Bring to the boil
and simmer, stirring, until thick,
then stir in the milk and cream
with salt and pepper to taste. Pour
into the pie dish and leave for
about 30 minutes until cold.

6 Roll out the pastry on a
floured work surface until
about 2.5 cm (1 inch) larger all
round than the pie dish.

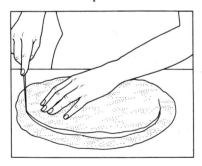

7 Cut off a strip from all round
the edge of the pastry. Place
the strip on the moistened rim of
the pie dish, moisten the strip,
then place the pastry lid on top.

8 Press the edge firmly to seal,
then knock up and flute. Make
a hole in the centre of the pie and
use the pastry trimmings to make
decorations, sticking them in place
with water.

9 Brush the pastry with beaten
egg, then bake in the oven at
190°C (375°F) mark 5 for 30
minutes until puffed up and
golden brown. Serve hot.

Menu Suggestion
Ideal for a midweek family meal,
this filling chicken pie needs no
further accompaniment other than
a freshly cooked green vegetable
such as French beans or spinach.

——— VARIATIONS ———

Replace the leeks with **6 sticks of
celery**, cleaned and cut in the
same way. Add them to the pan 3
minutes after adding the carrots.

Replace all of the leeks with **8
Jerusalem artichokes**, peeled
and thickly sliced.

Replace one of the carrots with
1 medium turnip, peeled and
roughly cubed.

Replace the carrots with **1
medium celeriac**, peeled and
cubed.

Replace the puff pastry with the
same weight of shortcrust pastry.

Add **100 g (4 oz) thickly sliced
mushrooms** and **5 ml (1
teaspoon) celery seeds** at step 5
when frying the onion.

STIR-FRIED CHICKEN WITH WALNUTS

0.20*	358 cals

* plus at least 1 hour marinating

Serves 4

4 boneless chicken breasts,
  skinned and cut into thin strips

5-cm (2-inch) piece of fresh root
  ginger, peeled and thinly sliced

60 ml (4 tbsp) soy sauce

60 ml (4 tbsp) dry sherry

5 ml (1 tsp) five-spice powder

45 ml (3 tbsp) sesame or vegetable
  oil

30 ml (2 tbsp) cornflour

150 ml ($\frac{1}{4}$ pint) chicken stock

salt and freshly ground pepper

75 g (3 oz) walnut pieces

$\frac{1}{4}$ cucumber, cut into chunks

spring onion tassels, to garnish

1 Put the chicken in a bowl with the ginger, soy sauce, sherry and five-spice powder. Stir well to mix, then cover and marinate for at least 1 hour.

2 Remove the chicken and ginger from the marinade with a slotted spoon. Reserve marinade.

3 Heat 30 ml (2 tbsp) of the oil in a wok or large heavy-based frying pan. Add the chicken and stir-fry over brisk heat for 5 minutes until well browned.

4 Mix the marinade with the cornflour then stir in the stock. Pour into the pan and bring to the boil, then add salt and pepper to taste and stir-fry for a further 5 minutes or until the chicken strips are tender.

5 Heat the remaining oil in a separate small pan, add the walnuts and cucumber and stir-fry briefly to heat through.

6 Transfer the chicken mixture to a warmed serving dish and top with the walnuts and cucumber. Garnish with spring onion tassels and serve.

Menu Suggestion
Serve with Chinese egg noodles, followed by a mixed salad of beansprouts, grated carrot, chopped celery and onion tossed in a dressing of oil, lemon juice and soy sauce.

CHICKEN FLORENTINE

1.00	527 cals

Serves 4

450 g (1 lb) fresh spinach

salt and freshly ground pepper

4 boneless chicken breasts, skinned

75 g (3 oz) butter or margarine

15 ml (1 tbsp) vegetable oil

1.25 ml ($\frac{1}{4}$ tsp) freshly grated nutmeg

25 g (1 oz) flour

450 ml ($\frac{3}{4}$ pint) milk

100 g (4 oz) Cheddar or Double Gloucester cheese, grated

pinch of ground mace

a little paprika

1 Wash the spinach, put into a pan with a pinch of salt. Cook over low heat for 7 minutes until just tender. Drain well.

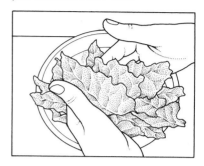

2 Meanwhile, cut each chicken breast in two horizontally. Melt 25 g (1 oz) of the fat in a frying pan with the oil. Fry the chicken for 3 minutes on each side.

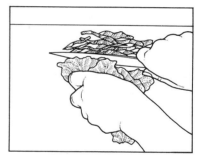

3 Chop the drained spinach. Mix with half of the remaining fat, the nutmeg and salt and pepper to taste. Put the spinach in the base of an ovenproof dish, then arrange the chicken on top.

4 Melt the remaining fat in a pan. Add the flour and stir for 2 minutes. Gradually add the milk, then the cheese, mace and seasoning. Simmer until thick.

5 Pour over the chicken, then sprinkle with the remaining cheese and a little paprika. Bake at 190°C (375°F) mark 5 for 30 minutes.

Menu Suggestion

Serve with mashed potatoes.

CHICKEN CROQUETTES

0.20*	✳*	642 cals

* plus 30 minutes cooling and at least
2–3 hours chilling; freeze after step 3

Serves 2

| 50 g (2 oz) butter or margarine |
| 60 ml (4 tbsp) flour |
| 200 ml ($\frac{1}{3}$ pint) milk |
| $\frac{1}{2}$ lemon |
| 15 ml (1 tbsp) capers, chopped |
| 175 g (6 oz) cooked chicken, minced |
| 15 ml (1 tbsp) chopped fresh parsley |
| salt and freshly ground pepper |
| 1 egg, beaten |
| 50 g (2 oz) dry white breadcrumbs |
| vegetable oil, for frying |
| lemon wedges, to garnish |

1 Melt the fat in a saucepan. Add the flour and cook gently, stirring, for 3 minutes. Remove from the heat and gradually stir in the milk. Bring to the boil and cook for about 5 minutes, stirring all the time, until the sauce is smooth and thick.

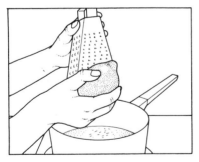

2 Grate in the lemon rind. Add the capers and chicken with the parsley and seasoning. Mix well together. Cool for 30 minutes, then chill in the refrigerator for 2–3 hours or preferably overnight.

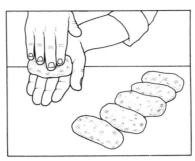

3 Shape the mixture into six even-sized croquettes. Dip in the beaten egg, then roll in the breadcrumbs to coat.

4 Deep-fry at 180°C (350°F) or shallow fry in hot oil for about 10 minutes or until golden brown. Serve hot, with lemon wedges.

Menu Suggestion
Serve Chicken Croquettes hot with French fries and a colourful medley of mixed vegetables such as peas, sweetcorn and red peppers, or a tomato salad.

CHICKEN CROQUETTES
Croquettes come in all shapes and sizes. Although they are most often made into sausage shapes as here, you can also try making them into rectangles, balls, egg shapes or flat cakes. Traditionally, they were often served as an entrée, or made very small and used as a garnish for roast meat or game.

The basic mixture can be varied by replacing the sauce with egg-enriched rice or potato purée, seasoned and mixed with any variety of flavourings and finely chopped or minced meat, fish or vegetable. Croquettes can also be made from thin pancakes stuffed and rolled up, then sliced, dipped in egg and bread-crumbs and deep-fried.

CHICKEN AND VEGETABLE RISOTTO

1.30	559 cals

Serves 4

| 175 g (6 oz) carrots, peeled |
| 225 g (8 oz) turnips, peeled |
| 175 g (6 oz) brown rice |
| 350 ml (12 fl oz) chicken stock |
| 50 g (2 oz) butter or margarine |
| 4 chicken quarters, halved, about 900 g (2 lb) total weight |
| 2 medium onions, skinned and chopped |
| 1 stick of celery, chopped |
| 50 g (2 oz) lean streaky bacon, rinded |
| salt and freshly ground pepper |
| 90 ml (6 tbsp) dry white wine |
| chopped fresh parsley, to garnish |

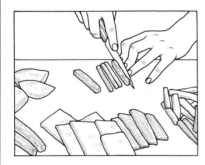

1 With a small sharp knife, cut the carrot and turnip into thick, even matchstick strips.

2 In a large saucepan, combine the rice and stock. Bring to the boil, then cover the pan and simmer for 15 minutes.

3 Melt 25 g (1 oz) fat in a flame-proof casserole. Add the chicken portions and fry for about 10 minutes until well browned. Remove from the pan.

4 Melt the remaining fat in the casserole, add all the vegetables and cook for 5 minutes until brown. Snip the bacon into the pan with kitchen scissors and fry gently for a further 2 minutes.

5 Stir in the rice mixture and season well. Arrange the chicken portions on top of the rice and vegetables. Spoon over the white wine.

6 Cover the casserole tightly with the lid or foil, then bake in the oven at 180°C (350°F) mark 4 for about 1 hour until the chicken is tender.

7 Just before serving, fork up the rice and vegetables round the chicken. Taste and adjust seasoning, then serve immediately, garnished with chopped parsley.

Menu Suggestion
Brown rice, chicken, bacon and vegetables make this risotto a substantial meal in itself. Serve for an informal family supper with hot garlic or herb bread, followed by a crisp mixed salad.

CHICKEN LIVER BOLOGNESE

0.40	835 cals

Serves 4

| 2 medium onions, skinned |
| 125 g (4 oz) carrots, peeled |
| 125 g (4 oz) celery |
| 50 g (2 oz) lard |
| 125 g (4 oz) streaky bacon, rinded |
| 450 g (1 lb) chicken livers, chopped |
| 45 ml (3 tbsp) tomato purée |
| 150 ml ($\frac{1}{4}$ pint) red wine |
| 150 ml ($\frac{1}{4}$ pint) chicken stock |
| 2.5 ml ($\frac{1}{2}$ tsp) dried oregano |
| 1 bay leaf |
| salt and freshly ground pepper |
| 275 g (10 oz) spaghetti |
| 25 g (1 oz) butter, melted |
| grated Parmesan cheese, to serve |

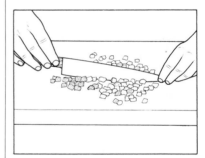

1 Chop the onions, carrots and celery finely. Melt the lard in a deep frying pan and fry the chopped vegetables until golden.

2 Snip the bacon into the pan, add the chicken livers and fry for about 5 minutes until the livers are browned on the outside and pink, but set, inside.

3 Stir in the tomato purée, red wine and stock. Add the oregano, bay leaf and seasoning, then bring to the boil. Lower heat, cover and simmer for 20 minutes.

4 Cook the spaghetti in boiling salted water for about 11 minutes until it is tender.

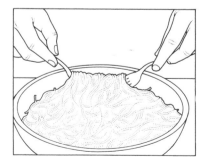

5 Drain the spaghetti and toss in
the melted butter. Season with
pepper. Serve with the chicken
liver sauce, and grated Parmesan.

Menu Suggestion
Serve with a green salad, and
chunks of French bread.

—— VARIATIONS ——

Instead of serving with pasta, use
the chicken liver mixture as a
filling for a herb-flavoured rice
ring and serve with a tomato
sauce handed separately. Or,
spoon the mixture into puff pastry
vol-au-vents or hot bread
croustades, and serve as a starter
or light main course.
   To make bread croustades,
choose a slightly stale unsliced

white loaf. Cut into 5 cm (2 inch)
thick rounds, 7.5 cm (3 inches) in
diameter. Using a smaller cutter,
cut through almost to the base,
then carefully hollow out the
centre. Place the rounds on a
buttered baking sheet and brush
with melted butter. Bake in the
oven at 170°C (325°F) mark 3 for
40 minutes, turning occasionally,
until crisp and brown all over.

Turkey Tetrazzini

| 1.00 | 449 cals |

Serves 6

225 g (8 oz) spaghetti
salt and freshly ground pepper
75 g (3 oz) butter or margarine
45 ml (3 tbsp) flour
300 ml ($\frac{1}{2}$ pint) hot homemade
  turkey or chicken stock (see
  page 157)
100 ml (4 fl oz) double cream
45 ml (3 tbsp) dry sherry
1.25 ml ($\frac{1}{4}$ tsp) freshly grated
  nutmeg
100 g (4 oz) button mushrooms,
  sliced
350–450 g (12–16 oz) cooked turkey,
  sliced or cut into bite-size
  pieces
30 ml (2 tbsp) grated Parmesan
  cheese

1 Cook the spaghetti in boiling salted water for about 11 minutes until it is just tender.

2 Meanwhile, make the sauce. Melt half the fat in a heavy-based saucepan, sprinkle in the flour and stir over gentle heat for 1–2 minutes. Stir in the hot stock gradually, then bring to the boil. Simmer, stirring all the time, until thick and smooth.

3 Remove the sauce from the heat and leave to cool for about 5 minutes, then stir in the cream, sherry, nutmeg and salt and pepper to taste.

4 Melt the remaining fat in a separate pan. Add the mushrooms and fry gently until soft.

5 Drain the spaghetti and arrange half of it in the base of a greased baking dish.

6 Arrange the turkey and mushrooms over the top. Cover with the remaining spaghetti, then coat with the sauce.

7 Sprinkle with the Parmesan and bake in the oven at 190°C (375°F) mark 5 for 30 minutes until golden and bubbling.

Menu Suggestion
Turkey Tetrazzini is a rich and filling American dish. Serve with a simple green or tomato salad.

QUICK TURKEY CURRY

| 0.45 | ✳ | 288–433 cals |

Serves 4–6

30 ml (2 tbsp) vegetable oil

3 bay leaves

2 cardamom pods, crushed

1 cinnamon stick, broken into short lengths

1 medium onion, skinned and thinly sliced

1 green pepper, cored, seeded and chopped (optional)

10 ml (2 tsp) paprika

7.5 ml (1½ tsp) garam masala

2.5 ml (½ tsp) turmeric

2.5 ml (½ tsp) chilli powder

salt and freshly ground pepper

50 g (2 oz) unsalted cashew nuts

700 g (1½ lb) turkey fillets, skinned and cut into bite-size pieces

2 medium potatoes, blanched, peeled and cut into chunks

4 tomatoes, skinned and chopped, or 225-g (8-oz) can tomatoes

bay leaves, to garnish

1 Heat the oil in a flameproof casserole, add the bay leaves, cardamom and cinnamon and fry over moderate heat for 1–2 minutes. Add the onion and green pepper (if using), with the spices and salt and pepper to taste. Pour in enough water to moisten, then stir to mix for 1 minute.

2 Add the cashews and turkey, cover and simmer for 20 minutes. Turn the turkey occasionally during this time to ensure even cooking.

3 Add the potatoes and tomatoes and continue cooking a further 20 minutes until the turkey and potatoes are tender. Taste and adjust seasoning before serving. Garnish with bay leaves.

Menu Suggestion
Serve with boiled rice, poppadoms, mango chutney and a yogurt and cucumber salad (raita).

QUICK TURKEY CURRY

The subtle blend of spices gives this a medium hot taste, without being too fiery! Chilli powder should be used with caution, since it is intensely hot.

Garam masala is readily available from Indian shops, specialist stores and some supermarkets. However, if you'd like to make your own, you will need about 100 g (4 oz) mixed large and small green cardamoms, 50 g (2 oz) cumin seeds, 15 g (½ oz) each black peppercorns, cloves and stick cinnamon and a little grated nutmeg. Dry-fry the whole spices for a few minutes, then grind together, mix in the nutmeg and store in an airtight container.

BAKED TURKEY ESCALOPES WITH CRANBERRY AND COCONUT

| 0.50 | 🗌 ✳* | 391 cals |

* freeze after step 2

Serves 4

| 450 g (1 lb) boneless turkey breast |
| salt and freshly ground pepper |
| 20 ml (4 tsp) Dijon mustard |
| 60 ml (4 tbsp) cranberry sauce |
| 15 g ($\frac{1}{2}$ oz) flour |
| 1 egg, beaten |
| 15 g ($\frac{1}{2}$ oz) desiccated coconut |
| 40 g (1$\frac{1}{2}$ oz) fresh breadcrumbs |
| 50 g (2 oz) butter or margarine |

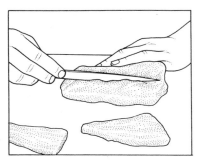

1 Thinly slice the turkey breast to give four portions.

2 Bat out the escalopes between two sheets of damp grease-proof paper or cling film. Season, then spread each portion with mustard and cranberry sauce.

3 Roll up, starting from the thin end, and secure with a cocktail stick or toothpick. Dust each portion with flour, then brush with egg. Combine the coconut and breadcrumbs then coat the turkey with the mixture.

4 Melt the fat in a frying pan, add the turkey portions, and fry until brown on both sides. Transfer to a baking tin just large enough to take the turkey in a single layer and baste with more fat. Bake in the oven at 180°C (350°F) mark 4 for about 40 minutes until tender.

Menu Suggestion

Serve these scrumptiously crisp escalopes with a salad of chopped and grated raw vegetables (e.g. celery, peppers, white cabbage, carrot and onion) tossed in a mayonnaise, soured cream or yogurt dressing. Alternatively, serve with a simple green salad.

BAKED TURKEY ESCALOPES WITH CRANBERRY AND COCONUT

Cranberries are a distinctively sharp-tasting fruit which make a delicious sauce, used here to add zest to turkey meat. The fresh fruit have a limited season, but they can also be bought frozen or canned throughout the year. Cultivated mainly in America, the ruby red berries grow on vines in flooded marshy soil. To harvest them, the water is whipped up by a machine. This dislodges the fruit which floats to the surface and is separated off from the leaves and other debris. The sorting process in-cludes a special machine which bounces the berries over a barrier seven times—if the berries don't bounce they are rejected as unsound!

Cranberry sauce is good mixed with fresh orange juice and poured over vanilla ice-cream, sweet pancakes or waffles, and whole berries are good in beef and pork casseroles.

STUFFED TURKEY LEGS

2.00	🗗	459 cals

Serves 6

2 turkey legs (drumsticks), at least 900 g (2 lb) total weight

225 g (8 oz) pork sausagemeat

15 ml (1 tbsp) chopped fresh tarragon or 2.5 ml ($\frac{1}{2}$ tsp) dried tarragon

10 ml (2 tsp) chopped fresh parsley

salt and freshly ground pepper

50 g (2 oz) button mushrooms, sliced

25 g (1 oz) flour

1 egg white, beaten

175 g (6 oz) fresh white breadcrumbs

100 g (4 oz) butter or margarine, softened

15 ml (1 tbsp) French mustard

watercress, to garnish

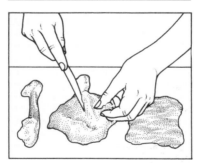

1 Skin the turkey legs, slit the flesh and carefully ease out the bone and large sinews.

2 Mix the sausagemeat, herbs and seasoning, and spread one quarter of the mixture over each boned leg. Cover with a layer of sliced mushrooms, then top with more sausagemeat stuffing.

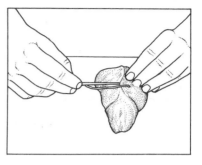

3 Reshape the stuffed turkey legs, then sew them up neatly, using fine string.

4 Dip the legs in flour, brush with beaten egg white and place seam side down in a greased roasting tin.

5 Beat together the breadcrumbs, butter and mustard. Spread over the tops and sides only of the legs.

6 Bake in the oven at 190°C (375°F) mark 5 for about 1 hour 40 minutes, until tender with a crisp, golden crust. Remove the string, slice, and serve with gravy made from the pan juices. Garnish with a sprig of watercress.

Menu Suggestion
Serve these roasted turkey legs sliced, as an unusual alternative to the traditional Sunday roast, with vegetables, roast potatoes and gravy made from the turkey's cooking juices.

Entertaining

When it's time to
entertain, you'll find
chicken and poultry so
versatile. Combined with
wine and cream they
become sumptuously
rich; with fruit they're
tangily different, with
herbs and spices instantly
something special.
Chicken is always
popular, but why not try
a more unusual bird?
Capon, duck, turkey,
guinea fowl, poussin and
quail are all widely
available, and
exceptionally good
quality. With their juicily
succulent flesh and subtle
flavours, and a chapter
full of new recipe ideas to
choose from, you simply
can't go wrong.

Spiced Chicken with Cashew Nuts

| 0.30* | 244 cals |

* plus 24 hours marinating

Serves 8

8 boneless chicken breasts, each
    weighing 75–100 g (3–4 oz),
    skinned

15 g (½ oz) fresh root ginger, peeled
    and roughly chopped

5 ml (1 tsp) coriander seeds

4 cloves

10 ml (2 tsp) black peppercorns

284 ml (10 oz) natural yogurt

1 medium onion, skinned and
    roughly chopped

50 g (2 oz) cashew nuts

2.5 ml (½ tsp) chilli powder

10 ml (2 tsp) turmeric

150 ml (¼ pint) water

40 g (1½ oz) ghee or clarified butter

salt

cashew nuts, chopped and toasted,
    and chopped fresh coriander, to
    garnish

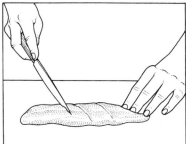

1 Make shallow slashes across
each of the chicken breasts.

2 Put the ginger in a blender or
food processor with the coriander seeds, cloves, peppercorns
and natural yogurt and work until
blended to a paste.

3 Pour the yogurt mixture over
the chicken, cover and marinate for about 24 hours, turning
the chicken once.

4 Put the onion in a blender or
food processor with the
cashew nuts, chilli powder, turmeric and water. Blend to a paste.

5 Lift the chicken out of the
marinade. Heat the ghee or
butter in a large sauté pan, add the
chicken pieces and fry until
browned on both sides.

6 Stir in the marinade with the
nut mixture and bring slowly
to the boil. Season with salt. Cover
the pan and simmer for about 20
minutes or until the chicken is
tender, stirring occasionally. Taste
and adjust seasoning and garnish
with cashew nuts and coriander
just before serving.

Menu Suggestion

Serve for an informal dinner party
with buttered noodles or rice and a
vegetable dish such as courgettes
and mushrooms tossed together in
garlic butter.

SPICED CHICKEN WITH CASHEW NUTS

In traditional Indian cookery,
ghee is often used to fry foods,
as in this recipe. The advantage
of using ghee rather than other
fats is that it can be heated to a
higher temperature without
catching and burning, and at the
same time it gives a good flavour.
You can buy ghee (which is
clarified butter) from Asian
stores, or make your own
clarified butter by heating 225 g
(8 oz) unsalted butter in a pan
until it melts. Simmer until clear
and a creamy residue settles in
the base of the pan. Remove
from the heat, spoon off the
foam on top and leave to cool.
Strain off the clear fat (ghee) from
the top and discard the residue.

CHICKEN VÉRONIQUE

1.45 | 342 cals

Serves 4

50 g (2 oz) butter

15 ml (1 tbsp) chopped fresh
tarragon or 10 ml (2 tsp) dried
tarragon

finely grated rind of 1 lemon

1 garlic clove, skinned and crushed

salt and freshly ground pepper

1.5 kg (3 lb) chicken

300 ml ($\frac{1}{2}$ pint) homemade chicken
stock (see page 157)

150 ml ($\frac{1}{4}$ pint) dry white wine

150 ml (5 fl oz) double cream

175 g (6 oz) green grapes, halved
and seeded

1 Soften the butter in a bowl
with the tarragon, lemon rind,
garlic and salt and pepper to taste.
Put half the mixture in the cavity
of the bird.

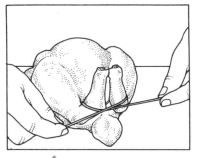

2 Truss the chicken with thread
or fine string. Spread the remainder of the mixture over the
outside of the bird (especially the
legs), then stand on a rack in a
roasting tin. Pour the chicken
stock under the rack.

3 Roast the chicken in the oven
at 200°C (400°F) mark 6 for
about 1$\frac{1}{4}$ hours or until the juices
run clear when the thickest part of
the thigh is pierced with a skewer.
Turn the bird and baste every 15
minutes or so during roasting.

4 Carve the chicken into neat
portions (see page 154), then
arrange on a warmed serving
platter, cover and keep warm.

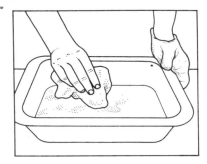

5 Make the sauce. Blot off any
excess fat from the roasting tin
with absorbent kitchen paper, then
place the tin on top of the cooker.
Pour in the wine, then boil to
reduce to about half the original
volume, stirring and scraping the
tin to dislodge sediment.

6 Stir in the cream and continue
simmering and stirring until
thick, smooth and glossy. Add the
grapes and heat through, then
taste and adjust seasoning.

7 Pour a little of the sauce over
the chicken, arranging the
grapes as attractively as possible
on each portion. Serve immediately, with the remaining
sauce and grapes handed
separately in a sauceboat.

Menu Suggestion
A rich and creamy main course for
a dinner party, Chicken Véronique
needs an accompaniment which
contrasts in flavour and texture.
Crisply cooked mange-touts or
French beans are ideal, with a
simple dish of plain boiled rice.
Serve with chilled dry white wine.

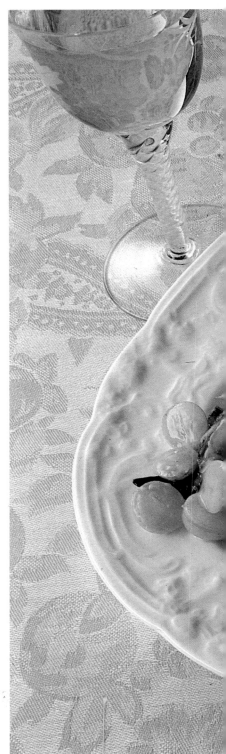

PÂTÉ CHICKEN

0.50	£	419 cals

Serves 4

15 g (½ oz) butter

10 ml (2 tsp) vegetable oil

4 chicken portions

5 ml (1 tsp) chopped fresh
   rosemary or 2.5 ml (½ tsp) dried
   rosemary

salt and freshly ground pepper

60 ml (4 tbsp) dry white wine

90 ml (6 tbsp) homemade chicken
   stock (see page 157)

50 g (2 oz) fine liver pâté

45 ml (3 tbsp) single cream

few sautéed sliced button
   mushrooms, to garnish

1 Heat the butter with the oil in a large frying pan. Add the chicken portions, sprinkle with the rosemary and salt and pepper to taste, then fry over moderate heat for 15–20 minutes until well coloured on all sides.

2 Pour in half the wine and half the stock, bring to the boil, then lower the heat, cover the pan and continue cooking a further 10–15 minutes until the chicken is tender. Remove the chicken from the pan with a slotted spoon.

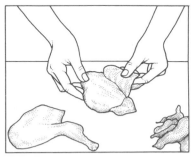

3 Strip the skin off the chicken portions and discard. Place the chicken on a serving platter, cover and keep hot while making sauce.

4 Add the remaining wine and stock to the pan and stir to combine with the cooking juices. Boil vigorously for a few minutes to reduce the liquid slightly.

5 Meanwhile, beat the pâté and cream together until they are smooth and well combined.

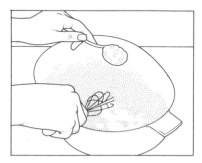

6 Gradually whisk the pâté mixture into the pan over low heat. Cook gently for 1–2 minutes, stirring constantly, then taste and adjust seasoning. Pour over the chicken, garnish with a few sautéed mushrooms and serve immediately.

Menu Suggestion
Quick to make, this chicken dish is perfect for last-minute entertaining. Serve with buttered noodles and finely sliced courgettes tossed in butter and lime or lemon juice.

NORMANDY CHICKEN

| 1.20 | £ £ | 622 cals |

Serves 4

30 ml (2 tbsp) vegetable oil
40 g (1½ oz) butter
4 chicken portions
6 eating apples
salt and freshly ground pepper
300 ml (½ pint) dry cider
60 ml (4 tbsp) Calvados
60 ml (4 tbsp) double cream
  (optional)

1 Heat the oil with 25 g (1 oz) of the butter in a large flame-proof casserole. Add the chicken portions and fry over moderate heat until golden brown on all sides. Remove from the pan and drain on absorbent kitchen paper.

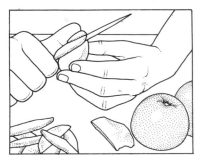

2 Peel, core and slice four of the apples. Add to the pan and fry gently, tossing constantly, until lightly coloured.

3 Return the chicken portions to the pan, placing them on top of the apples. Sprinkle with salt and pepper to taste, then pour in the cider. Bring to the boil, then cover and cook in the oven at 180°C (350°F) mark 4 for 45 minutes or until the chicken portions are tender.

4 Meanwhile, peel, core and slice the remaining apples. Melt the 15 g (½ oz) butter in a frying pan, add the apple slices and toss to coat in the fat. Fry until lightly coloured, then spoon over chicken.

5 Warm the Calvados gently in a ladle or small pan, then ignite and pour over the chicken and apples. Serve as soon as the flames have died down, drizzled with cream, if liked.

Menu Suggestion
Calvados and cider combine together to make this main course dish quite heady. Serve with plain boiled potatoes sprinkled with melted butter and chopped fresh herbs, with a green salad tossed in a sharp vinaigrette dressing to follow. French dry cider would make an unusual drink to serve instead of wine.

Chicken Marengo

| 1.25 | ✳ | 757 cals |

Serves 4

4 chicken portions
50 g (2 oz) flour
100 ml (4 fl oz) olive oil
50 g (2 oz) butter
1 medium onion, skinned and sliced
30 ml (2 tbsp) brandy
salt and freshly ground pepper
450 g (1 lb) tomatoes, skinned, or 397-g (14-oz) can tomatoes, with their juice
1 garlic clove, skinned and crushed
150 ml (¼ pint) chicken stock
100 g (4 oz) button mushrooms
chopped fresh parsley, to garnish

1 Coat the chicken portions in the flour. Heat the oil in a large frying pan and fry the chicken on both sides, until golden brown, about 5–10 minutes. Remove from the frying pan and place, skin side up, in a large saucepan or flameproof casserole together with 25 g (1 oz) butter.

2 Add the onion to the oil in the frying pan and cook for 5 minutes until soft.

3 Sprinkle the chicken joints with the brandy and salt and pepper and turn the joints over.

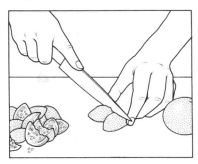

4 Roughly chop the tomatoes. Add them to the chicken with the onion, garlic and stock. Cover and simmer gently for about 1 hour, until the chicken is tender.

5 Ten minutes before serving, melt the remaining butter in a pan and cook the mushrooms for about 5 minutes, until soft. Drain and add to the chicken.

6 When the chicken joints are cooked, remove to a warmed serving dish. If the sauce is too thin, boil briskly to reduce. Spoon the sauce over the chicken and serve garnished with parsley.

Menu Suggestion
A classic French dish with its own sauce, Chicken Marengo should be served with steamed or boiled new potatoes and a green salad to follow.

MIDDLE EASTERN STUFFED CHICKEN

2.40	415 cals

Serves 6

75 g (3 oz) butter

1 small onion, skinned and finely
  chopped

1–2 garlic cloves, skinned and
  crushed

50 g (2 oz) blanched almonds,
  roughly chopped

50 g (2 oz) long grain rice

150 ml (¼ pint) water

salt and freshly ground pepper

50 g (2 oz) stoned prunes, chopped

50 g (2 oz) dried apricots, chopped

2.5 ml (½ tsp) ground cinnamon

1.8 kg (4 lb) chicken

1 Melt one third of the butter
in a heavy-based saucepan,
add the onion and garlic and fry
gently until soft and lightly
coloured. Add the almonds and
fry until turning colour, then add
the rice and stir-fry until the
grains begin to swell and burst.

2 Pour the water over the rice
(it will bubble furiously), then
add salt and pepper to taste. Cover
and simmer for 15 minutes or
until all the water has been absorbed by the rice.

3 Remove the pan from the heat
and stir in 25 g (1 oz) butter
with the dried fruit and cinnamon.
Taste and adjust the seasoning.

4 Stuff the chicken with the rice
mixture, then truss with
thread or fine string. Place on a
large sheet of foil and brush with
the remaining butter. Sprinkle
liberally with salt and pepper,
then wrap tightly in the foil.

5 Roast in the oven at 200°C
(400°F) mark 6 for 1½ hours,
then unwrap and roast for a
further 30 minutes until the
chicken is brown and the juices
run clear when the thickest part
of the thigh is pierced with a
skewer. Serve hot.

Menu Suggestion
Serve with saffron rice.

CHICKEN CORDON BLEU

0.45* ⬜ ✳* 452 cals

* plus 30 minutes chilling; freeze after step 5

Serves 4

4 boneless chicken breasts, skinned
4 thin slices of boiled ham
4 thin slices of Gruyère cheese
salt and freshly ground pepper
about 25 g (1 oz) flour
1 egg, beaten
75 g (3 oz) dried white breadcrumbs
60 ml (4 tbsp) vegetable oil
50 g (2 oz) butter
lemon twists and sprigs of fresh herbs, to garnish

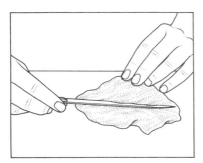

1 Slit along one long edge of each chicken breast, then carefully work knife to the opposite edge, using a sawing action.

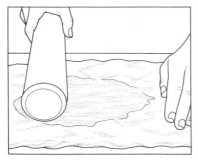

2 Open out the chicken breast, place between two sheets of damp greaseproof paper or cling film and beat with a meat bat or rolling pin to flatten slightly.

3 Place a slice of ham on top of each piece of chicken, then a slice of cheese. Fold the chicken over to enclose ham and cheese.

4 Pound the open edge of the parcels so that they stay together, then secure with wooden cocktail sticks.

5 Sprinkle the chicken parcels with salt and pepper to taste, then coat lightly in flour. Dip in the beaten egg, then in the breadcrumbs. Press the breadcrumbs on firmly so that they adhere evenly and completely coat the chicken. Refrigerate for about 30 minutes.

6 Heat the oil and butter together in a large heavy-based frying pan (you may need to use two if the chicken parcels are large), then fry the chicken for 10 minutes on each side until crisp and golden. Drain on absorbent paper, remove the cocktail sticks, then arrange the chicken on a warmed serving platter and garnish with lemon and herbs.

Menu Suggestion
Crunchy on the outside, meltingly delicious on the inside, Chicken Cordon Bleu goes well with vegetables such as mushrooms, or French beans, spinach, courgettes and mange-touts. Sauté potatoes can also be served, for hungry guests!

Turkey Sauté with Lemon and Walnuts

0.20	383 cals

Serves 4

450 g (1 lb) turkey breast steaks
30 ml (2 tbsp) cornflour
1 green pepper
30 ml (2 tbsp) vegetable oil
40 g (1½ oz) walnut halves or pieces
25 g (1 oz) butter or margarine
60 ml (4 tbsp) chicken stock
30 ml (2 tbsp) lemon juice
45 ml (3 tbsp) lemon marmalade
5 ml (1 tsp) white wine vinegar
1.25 ml (¼ tsp) soy sauce
salt and freshly ground pepper

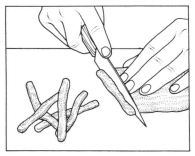

1 Cut up the turkey flesh into 5-cm (2-inch) pencil thin strips. Toss in the cornflour.

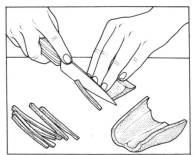

2 Slice the green pepper into fine strips, discarding the core and all the seeds.

3 Heat the oil in a large sauté or deep frying pan, add the walnuts and pepper strips and fry for 2–3 minutes. Remove from the pan with a slotted spoon.

4 Melt the fat in the residual oil and fry the turkey strips for 10 minutes until golden. Stir in the stock and lemon juice, stirring well to remove any sediment at the bottom of the pan. Add the lemon marmalade, vinegar, soy sauce and some salt and pepper.

5 Return the walnuts and green pepper to the pan. Cook gently for a further 5 minutes, until the turkey is tender. Taste and adjust seasoning and serve immediately.

Menu Suggestion

The subtle sweetness of this simple-to-make sauté dish gives it a most unusual flavour. Serve with a plain accompaniment such as boiled rice or Chinese egg noodles, so your guests can appreciate its flavour to the full.

TURKEY SAUTÉ

The French word sauté (literally 'to jump') has been adopted into the English language, and this method of quick cooking is now very popular.

Whatever food you choose to cook, the principles of sautéing are always the same—the meat is cut into fairly small pieces and tossed quickly in hot fat or oil. It is then cooked for the minimum amount of time with the other chosen ingredients and a dash of liquid to moisten the pan until the food is just tender. The whole process is easy, and it's a conveniently quick and tasty way of cooking.

TURKEY SCALOPPINE WITH ALMOND CREAM

| 0.30 | 🍴 | £ £ | 418 cals |

Serves 4

4 turkey steaks

30 ml (2 tbsp) lemon juice

salt and freshly ground pepper

30 ml (2 tbsp) vegetable oil

50 g (2 oz) blanched almonds, roughly chopped

30 ml (2 tbsp) brandy

150 ml (5 fl oz) single cream

1 garlic clove, skinned and crushed

snipped fresh chives, to garnish

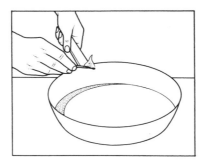

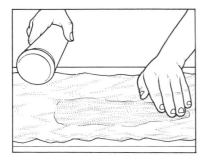

1 Bat out each turkey steak thinly between sheets of damp greaseproof paper or cling film. Divide each steak into three pieces. Place in a shallow dish and sprinkle over the lemon juice. Season and leave aside for 15 minutes to marinate.

2 Heat the oil in a sauté pan, add the almonds and fry until brown. Remove from the pan.

3 Add the turkey pieces and sauté for about 3 minutes on each side or until golden brown. Remove from the pan using a slotted spoon and keep warm.

4 Add the brandy to the pan, heat gently, then remove from the heat and ignite the brandy.

5 When the flames have died down, stir in the single cream, crushed garlic and the browned almonds. Return to the heat and warm through—do not boil. Pour the sauce over the turkey steaks and snip fresh chives over the top. Serve immediately.

Menu Suggestion
Quick and easy to make if you have to entertain unexpected guests, this dish contains a rich combination of turkey, almonds, brandy and cream. A lightly cooked vegetable such as broccoli would provide the perfect crisp contrast, with buttered new potatoes as an additional accompaniment.

--- VARIATIONS ---

Try using **chopped skinned hazelnuts** in place of the blanched almonds.

Replace the brandy with the same quantity of **dry sherry**.

Omit the crushed garlic clove and add a little **finely chopped fresh ginger root** to the pan instead.

TURKEY STROGANOFF

| 0.15 | 🍴 | 310 cals |

Serves 4

| 450 g (1 lb) turkey fillet |
| 15 ml (1 tbsp) vegetable oil |
| 50 g (2 oz) butter |
| 30 ml (2 tbsp) brandy |
| 1 garlic clove, skinned and crushed |
| salt and freshly ground pepper |
| 225 g (8 oz) button mushrooms, sliced |
| 1 green pepper, cored, seeded and sliced |
| 60 ml (4 tbsp) soured cream |

1 Slice the piece of turkey fillet into pencil-thin strips, using a sharp knife.

2 Heat the oil and butter in a large sauté pan and brown the turkey strips. Remove from the heat. Heat the brandy in a small pan, ignite and pour over the turkey. Return to the heat then add the garlic and seasoning.

3 Cover the pan and simmer for about 4–5 minutes or until the turkey is just tender.

4 Increase the heat, add the mushrooms and pepper and cook for 3–4 minutes, turning occasionally, until just softened.

5 Reduce the heat, stir in the soured cream, taste and adjust seasoning. Serve immediately.

Menu Suggestion
Serve on a bed of boiled white rice or buttered noodles, with a crisp green salad to follow.

DUCK WITH RASPBERRIES

| 0.40* | 🍳 | £ £ | 657 cals |

* plus 4 hours marinating

Serves 2

| 1.8–2.3 kg (4–5 lb) duckling |
| 30 ml (2 tbsp) brandy |
| juice of 2 limes |
| 30 ml (2 tbsp) clear honey |
| 10 ml (2 tsp) green peppercorns |
| salt and freshly ground pepper |
| 15 g ($\frac{1}{2}$ oz) butter |
| 30 ml (2 tbsp) vegetable oil |
| 225 g (8 oz) fresh or frozen raspberries |
| 300 ml ($\frac{1}{2}$ pint) rosé wine |
| blanched julienne shreds of lime zest, to garnish |

1 Remove the duck breasts. With a sharp knife cut along the length of one side of the breast bone as far as the wing joints. Ease the breast away from the carcass using short, sharp strokes and keeping the knife close to the bone. Remove the breast and repeat the process on the other side. Set the carcass aside.

2 Make the marinade. Mix together the brandy, lime juice and half the honey, with half the peppercorns, crushed, and salt and pepper to taste.

3 Remove the skin from the duck breasts, then place the breasts in a shallow dish. Pour over the marinade and leave to stand for 4 hours. Turn the duck in the marinade occasionally during this time.

4 Melt the butter with the oil in a frying pan. Remove the duck from the marinade, place in the pan and fry over high heat for a few minutes. Turn the breasts over, and cook for a further 5 minutes or until they are tender, but still slightly pink inside.

5 Meanwhile, put the raspberries in a heavy-based pan with the marinade and the wine. Heat gently for a few minutes, then remove about one quarter of the raspberries with a slotted spoon and set aside.

6 Add the remaining honey to the pan and boil until the liquid is reduced to about half.

7 Strain the sauce through a sieve, pressing the raspberries with the back of a spoon. Return to the rinsed-out pan with the reserved whole raspberries and reheat. Taste for sweetness and adjust seasoning.

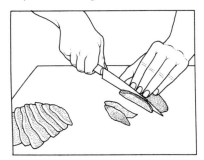

8 Slice the duck breasts neatly, then arrange on warmed individual serving plates. Pour over the sauce, then sprinkle with the remaining whole peppercorns. Garnish with lime julienne and serve immediately.

Menu Suggestion

A very special dinner party dish. Serve with *gratin dauphinois* (sliced potatoes baked with cream and Gruyère cheese) and a crisply cooked green vegetable such as mange-touts or French beans. Chilled rosé wine is the most suitable drink.

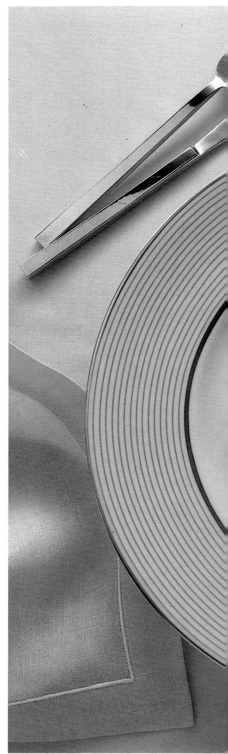

SWEET AND SOUR DUCK JOINTS

| 1.00 | 458 cals |

Serves 4

4 duck portions
salt and freshly ground pepper
60 ml (4 tbsp) soy sauce
45 ml (3 tbsp) soft brown sugar
45 ml (3 tbsp) honey
45 ml (3 tbsp) wine or cider vinegar
30 ml (2 tbsp) dry sherry
juice of 1 orange
150 ml ($\frac{1}{4}$ pint) water
2.5 ml ($\frac{1}{2}$ tsp) ground ginger
few orange slices and watercress
 sprigs, to garnish

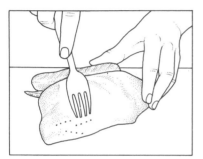

1 Prick the duck portions all over with a fork, then sprinkle the skin liberally with salt and freshly ground pepper.

2 Place on a rack in a roasting tin and roast in the oven at 190°C (375°F) mark 5 for 45–60 minutes until the skin is crisp and the juices run clear when the thickest part of each joint is pierced with a skewer.

3 Meanwhile, make the sauce. Mix together all the remaining ingredients in a saucepan and bring to the boil. Simmer, stirring constantly, for about 5 minutes to allow the flavours to blend and the sauce to thicken slightly. Add salt and pepper to taste.

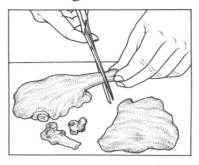

4 Trim the duck joints neatly by cutting off any knuckles or wing joints. Arrange the duck on a warmed serving platter and coat with some of the sauce. Garnish with orange and watercress. Hand remaining sauce separately.

Menu Suggestion
For an unusual Chinese-style meal, serve these duck joints with Chinese egg noodles and a stir-fried dish of finely sliced celery, onion and fresh root ginger with beansprouts, grated carrot and broccoli or cauliflower florets.

ROAST DUCK WITH GRAPEFRUIT

2.00* 🍴🍴 £ £ ✳ 524 cals

* plus 3–4 hours cooling and overnight chilling

Serves 8

125 g (4 oz) fresh white breadcrumbs

225 g (8 oz) minced pork

225 g (8 oz) minced veal

100 g (4 oz) cooked ham

8 stuffed green olives

1 small grapefruit

2.5 ml (½ tsp) dried sage or 5 ml (1 tsp) chopped fresh sage

salt and freshly ground pepper

1 egg

2 kg (4½ lb) duckling, boned (see page 153)

grapefruit slices, to garnish

1 Place the breadcrumbs, minced pork and veal in a large mixing bowl. Roughly chop the ham and olives and add to the mixture. Grate the rind of the grapefruit and chop the flesh. Add to the mixture with the sage, plenty of seasoning and the egg. Stir well until evenly blended.

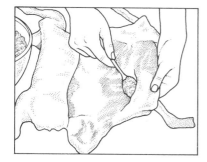

2 Spoon a little stuffing into each of the leg cavities of the duck, pressing in firmly.

3 Mound the remaining stuffing in the centre of the body section. Using a needle and fine string or cotton, sew up the body and wing cavities.

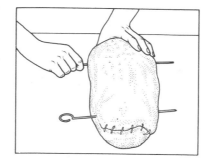

4 Turn the bird over, breast side up, then push it back into shape and secure with skewers.

5 Weigh the duckling and put on a wire rack placed over a roasting tin. Sprinkle with salt. Roast at 180°C (350°F) mark 4, allowing 25 minutes per 450 g (1 lb), basting occasionally. Pierce the duckling leg with a fine skewer; the juices should run clear when the bird is cooked. Leave for 3–4 hours until cool, then refrigerate overnight.

6 To serve, carefully ease out the string and slice. Garnish with the grapefruit slices.

Menu Suggestion

Serve with a selection of salads and chilled dry white wine or Champagne.

ITALIAN STUFFED CAPON

4.20* ⊟ ⊟ £ £ 378–504 cals

* plus 3–4 hours cooling and overnight chilling

Serves 12–16

100 g (4 oz) butter

1 medium onion, skinned and finely chopped

45 ml (3 tbsp) Marsala

50 g (2 oz) green olives

450 g (1 lb) minced pork

100 g (4 oz) fresh white breadcrumbs

50 g (2 oz) pine nuts, roughly chopped

15 ml (1 tbsp) chopped fresh marjoram or 5 ml (1 tsp) dried marjoram

pinch of grated nutmeg

salt and freshly ground pepper

1 egg, beaten

3 kg (6½ lb) capon, boned (see page 153)

450 g (1 lb) piece Italian salami, skinned

sprigs of watercress, to garnish

1 Melt 50 g (2 oz) of the butter in a frying pan and cook the onion for 5 minutes until soft but not brown. Add the Marsala and boil rapidly for 2 minutes. Cool slightly for 5 minutes.

2 Stone the olives, then roughly chop the flesh. Add to the onion with the minced pork, breadcrumbs, pine nuts, marjoram, nutmeg and salt and pepper to taste. Bind with the egg.

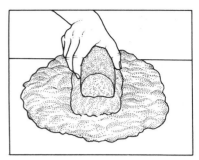

3 Place the capon, skin side down, on a large board or work surface. Push the legs and wings inside and bat out with a rolling pin to evenly distribute the flesh. Spread one half of the stuffing mixture over the centre of the capon, then place the salami on top. Cover with the remaining stuffing mixture.

4 Sew up the capon with fine string or strong thread, reshaping the bird. Weigh the bird.

5 Place the bird in a roasting tin. Sprinkle with salt and pepper, then spread with remaining butter. Roast in the oven at 190°C (375°F) mark 5, basting occasionally, allowing 25 minutes per 450 g (1 lb).

6 Cool completely for 3–4 hours, then refrigerate overnight. Remove string before slicing. Garnish with watercress.

Menu Suggestion
Serve this cold dish for a festive occasion with a rice salad and a tomato and basil salad.

SPATCHCOCKED GUINEA FOWL WITH PLUM AND GINGER SAUCE

| 1.00 | 🍳 | £ £ | 286 cals |

Serves 4

2 guinea fowl

50 g (2 oz) butter or margarine

1 shallot or 2 spring onions, skinned or trimmed and finely chopped

100 ml (4 fl oz) red wine

30 ml (2 tbsp) thick plum or damson jam

1.25 ml–2.5 ml ($\frac{1}{4}$–$\frac{1}{2}$ tsp) ground ginger, according to taste

salt and freshly ground pepper

30 ml (2 tbsp) crushed juniper berries

watercress sprigs, to garnish

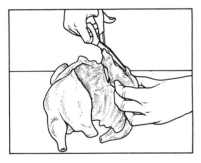

1 Prepare each guinea fowl for grilling. Cut off the wing tips. Remove the backbone by cutting down each side of it with scissors, then easing it out without cutting the bird in half.

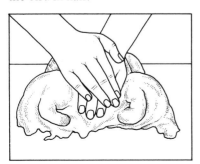

2 Turn the bird over and open it out. Snip the wishbone from the underside so that the bird can lie completely flat.

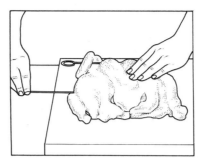

3 Push 2 skewers crossways into each bird, one through both legs and one through both wings.

4 Make the plum sauce. Melt half the fat in a small pan, add the shallot or spring onions and fry gently for 5 minutes until soft. Pour in the wine, then add the jam, ginger and salt and pepper to taste. Heat gently until the jam melts, then bring to the boil and simmer for a few minutes until thickened slightly. Remove from the heat.

5 Melt the remaining fat in a small pan with the juniper berries and salt and pepper to taste. Place the guinea fowl on an oiled grill and brush with half of the juniper berry mixture. Grill for 7 minutes, then turn the guinea fowl over and brush with the remaining mixture. Grill for a further 7 minutes.

6 To make sure the insides of the legs are cooked through, remove the skewers from the legs and fold the legs back so that they are exposed to the heat underneath. Grill for a further few minutes, covering the rest of the birds with foil if they are becoming too well browned.

7 Just before the guinea fowl are ready to serve, pour the cooking juices into the plum sauce and reheat. Taste and adjust seasoning. Remove the remaining skewers from the birds, then arrange them on a serving platter and garnish with watercress. Serve sauce separately in a sauceboat.

Menu Suggestion
Rich and very different, this main course game dish is best served with traditional vegetables such as creamed potatoes, and Brussels sprouts tossed with chestnuts and chopped thyme. A full-bodied red wine is the most suitable drink.

SPATCHCOCKED GUINEA FOWL

Nowadays guinea fowl are bred for the table, so these smallish birds are plumper than the wild guinea fowl. The tender flesh has a delicious flavour rather like gamy chicken, but it must be kept moist during cooking as it has a tendency to dry out.

Guinea fowl are available all year round and make an excellent choice for a special occasion. They can be roasted in the traditional way, or used in almost any recipe for pheasant, partridge or young chicken.

Older, slightly tougher birds may be casseroled successfully, to tenderise them.

DEVILLED POUSSINS

| 0.55* | 🗇 | 256 cals |

* plus 1–2 hours chilling

Serves 6

15 ml (1 tbsp) mustard powder

15 ml (1 tbsp) paprika

20 ml (4 tsp) turmeric

20 ml (4 tsp) ground cumin

60 ml (4 tbsp) tomato ketchup

15 ml (1 tbsp) lemon juice

75 g (3 oz) butter, melted

3 poussins, each weighing about 700 g (1½ lb)

15 ml (1 tbsp) poppy seeds

1 Measure the mustard powder, paprika, turmeric and cumin into a small bowl. Add the tomato ketchup and lemon juice. Beat well to form a thick, smooth paste. Slowly pour in the melted butter, stirring all the time.

2 Place the poussins on a chopping board, breast side down. With a small sharp knife cut right along the backbone of each bird through skin and flesh.

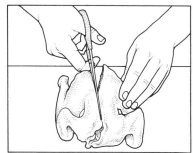

3 With scissors, cut through the backbone to open the birds up. Turn birds over, breast side up.

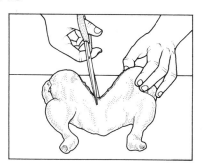

4 Continue cutting along the breast bone which will split the birds into two equal halves.

5 Lie the birds, skin side uppermost, on a large edged baking sheet. Spread the paste evenly over the surface of the birds and sprinkle with the poppy seeds. Cover loosely with cling film and leave in a cool place for at least 1–2 hours.

6 Cook the poussins (uncovered on the baking sheet) in the oven at 220°C (425°F) mark 7 for 15 minutes.

7 Remove from the oven and place under a hot grill until the skin is well browned and crisp.

8 Return to the oven, reduce temperature to 180°C (350°F) mark 4 and cook for a further 20 minutes until the poussins are tender. Serve immediately.

Menu Suggestion

Serve for an informal supper party with jacket baked potatoes topped with butter, crumbled crisp bacon, soured cream and chives. Serve ice-cold lager, beer or cider to drink, and follow with a refreshingly crisp salad of raw vegetables.

QUAIL COOKED WITH JUNIPER

0.35	£ £	353 cals

Serves 4

100 g (4 oz) butter
8 quail
salt
300 ml (½ pint) chicken stock
6 juniper berries, washed
30 ml (2 tbsp) gin or brandy
watercress, to garnish

1 Melt the butter in a large pan and fry the birds until brown on all sides.

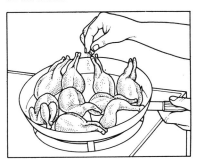

2 Sprinkle with salt. Cover the pan and cook over moderate heat for about 20 minutes. If pre-ferred, the birds can be cooked in the oven at 180°C (350°F) mark 4.

3 When the birds are nearly cooked, add the stock, juniper berries and gin or brandy. Con-tinue to cook for a further 10 minutes until the birds are tender.

4 To serve, put the birds on to a warmed large dish and pour the cooking liquid round them. Serve immediately, garnished with sprigs of watercress.

Menu Suggestion
Richly-flavoured quail needs con-trasting plain vegetables such as creamed potatoes, broccoli or cauliflower and French beans.

Great Dishes of The World

Tasty, lean and tender, chicken and poultry are popular meats in so many different countries of the world, and this chapter brings you a selection of some of the best classic recipes. Dishes from Russia, France, Greece, India, Catalonia, America, Japan, The Middle East, Mexico, Great Britain, China and Italy. Some for everyday family meals, others more suitable for entertaining guests—they're all here for you and your family and friends to savour and enjoy.

CHICKEN KIEV

| 0.45* | ⊟ | ✳* | 520 cals |

* plus 1 hour chilling; freeze after step 6

Serves 4

4 large boneless chicken breasts, skinned

100 g (4 oz) butter

finely grated rind of ½ a lemon

15 ml (1 tbsp) lemon juice

15 ml (1 tbsp) chopped fresh parsley

1 garlic clove, skinned and crushed

salt and freshly ground pepper

25 g (1 oz) flour

1 egg, beaten

100 g (4 oz) fresh white breadcrumbs

vegetable oil for deep-frying

1 Place the chicken breasts on a wooden board and pound them to an even thickness with a meat mallet or rolling pin.

2 Work the butter with the lemon rind and juice, the parsley, garlic and salt and pepper to taste.

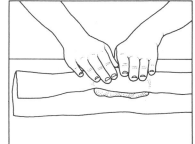

3 Place the butter on a sheet of non-stick or waxed paper and form into a roll. Refrigerate until the butter is firm.

4 Cut the butter into four pieces and place one piece on each of the flattened chicken breasts.

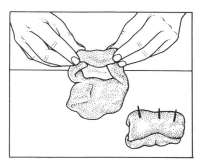

5 Roll up the chicken, folding the ends in to enclose the butter completely. Secure with wooden cocktail sticks.

6 Coat the chicken breasts in the flour seasoned with salt and pepper, then in beaten egg and breadcrumbs. Pat the crumbs firmly so that the chicken is well coated. Chill for at least 1 hour or until required.

7 Heat the oil to 170°C (325°F). Place two chicken portions in a frying basket and carefully lower into the oil; deep-fry for about 15 minutes, then drain on absorbent kitchen paper while frying the rest. Serve immediately.

Menu Suggestion
Crisp outside, oozing with garlic butter within, Chicken Kiev tastes good with sauté potatoes and a seasonal green vegetable, plus a Russian-style beetroot and soured cream salad.

COQ AU VIN

| 1.45 | ⌂ | £ £ | ✳ | 401–535 cals |

Serves 6–8

| 1 large roasting chicken or capon, cut into 8 joints (see page 151), or 6–8 chicken joints |
| 30 ml (2 tbsp) flour |
| salt and freshly ground pepper |
| 90 g (3½ oz) butter |
| 100 g (4 oz) lean bacon, diced |
| 1 medium onion, skinned and quartered |
| 1 carrot, peeled and quartered |
| 60 ml (4 tbsp) brandy |
| 600 ml (1 pint) red Burgundy wine |
| 1 garlic clove, skinned and lightly crushed |
| 1 bouquet garni |
| 30 ml (2 tbsp) vegetable oil |
| 450 g (1 lb) button onions, skinned |
| pinch of sugar |
| 5 ml (1 tsp)) wine vinegar |
| 225 g (8 oz) button mushrooms |
| 3 slices of white bread, crusts removed |
| chopped fresh parsley, to garnish |

1 Coat the chicken pieces with 15 ml (1 tbsp) of the flour, liberally seasoned with salt and freshly ground pepper.

2 Melt 25 g (1 oz) of the butter in a flameproof casserole, add the bacon, quartered onion and carrot and fry gently until the bacon begins to change colour. Add the chicken pieces, raise the heat and fry until they are golden brown on all sides.

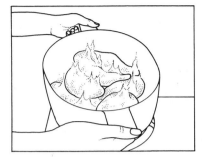

3 Heat the brandy in a small saucepan, set it alight and pour over the chicken, shaking the pan so that all the chicken pieces are covered in flames. When the flames have subsided, pour on the wine and stir to remove any sediment.

4 Add the garlic and bouquet garni. Bring to the boil, then cover and simmer very gently for 1 hour until the chicken is tender.

5 Meanwhile, melt another 25 g (1 oz) of the butter with 7.5 ml (½ tbsp) of the oil in a frying pan. Add the button onions and fry until they begin to brown. Add the sugar and vinegar, together with 15 ml (1 tbsp) of the cooking liquid. Cover and simmer for 10 minutes or until just tender. Keep warm.

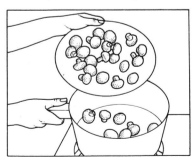

6 Melt 25 g (1 oz) of the butter with 7.5 ml (½ tbsp) of the oil in a heavy saucepan that is wide enough to hold the mushrooms lying flat. Raise the heat and add the mushrooms. Cook for about 5 minutes until they are crisp and lightly browned. Keep warm.

7 When cooked, lift the chicken pieces out of the casserole and place in a warmed deep serving dish. Discard the bouquet garni. Surround the chicken with the small onions and mushrooms and keep hot.

8 Drain the excess fat off the cooking liquid into a frying pan. Boil the liquid in the casserole briskly for about 3–5 minutes to reduce.

9 Add the remaining oil to the fat in the frying pan and quickly fry the pieces of bread until golden brown on both sides. Cut each slice into four triangles.

10 Work the remaining flour into the remaining butter. Take the casserole off the heat and add this beurre manié in small pieces to the cooking liquid. Stir until smooth, then bring just to the boil. The sauce should now be quite thick and shiny. Taste and adjust seasoning and pour over the chicken. Sprinkle with the chopped parsley and garnish with the fried bread.

Menu Suggestion
A casserole of chicken pieces in a heady red wine sauce with onions and mushrooms, Coq au Vin is best served with a French potato dish such as *gratin dauphinois* (sliced potatoes baked with cream and Gruyère cheese). Follow with a green salad tossed in vinaigrette dressing.

KOTOPOULO KAPANICI

1.00	£ £ ✳	416 cals

Serves 4

4 chicken portions, skinned

salt and freshly ground pepper

45 ml (3 tbsp) olive oil

15 g ($\frac{1}{2}$ oz) butter

1 small onion, skinned and chopped

3 garlic cloves, skinned and crushed

100 ml (4 fl oz) dry white wine

450 g (1 lb) ripe tomatoes, skinned, seeded and chopped

15 ml (1 tbsp) tomato purée

1 cinnamon stick

4 cloves

6 allspice berries

150 ml ($\frac{1}{4}$ pint) water

175-g (6-oz) can or jar artichoke hearts, drained (optional)

15–30 ml (1–2 tbsp) chopped fresh parsley or coriander

1 Sprinkle the chicken liberally with salt and pepper. Heat the oil with the butter in a large flame-proof casserole, add the chicken and fry over moderate heat for about 5 minutes until well coloured on all sides. Remove from the pan with a slotted spoon and set aside.

2 Add the onion and garlic to the pan and fry gently for about 5 minutes until soft.

3 Return the chicken to the pan, pour in the wine, then add the tomatoes and tomato purée and mix well. Let the mixture bubble for a few minutes.

4 Meanwhile, pound the spices with a pestle in a mortar. Add to the casserole with the water and stir well to mix. Cover the pan and simmer for about 45–60 minutes until the chicken is tender

5 Add the artichokes (if using) about 10 minutes before the end of cooking time, to heat through. Taste and adjust seasoning, stir in the parsley or coriander and serve immediately.

Menu Suggestion

This Greek chicken casserole with its spicy tomato sauce goes well with plain boiled rice or a Greek potato dish made by tossing new potatoes in their skins in a mixture of olive oil, white wine and crushed coriander seeds. Follow with a salad of raw shredded white cabbage and lettuce, sliced onion, black olives and crumbled Feta cheese tossed in an olive oil and lemon juice dressing.

KOTOPOULO KAPANICI

This spicy chicken casserole comes from Greece. The Greeks would choose a boiling fowl rather than a young chicken, which would be reserved for grilling, or any other quick method of cooking. The chicken is simmered gently in a rich tomato and wine mixture until very tender and juicy. What makes it different from other chicken casseroles is the addition of cinnamon, cloves and allspice which give the finished dish a distinctive warm and spicy flavour. Although all these spices are available ground, the flavour is far superior if you buy them whole and grind your own just before using.

Cinnamon is the aromatic bark of a type of laurel tree, native to India, while allspice 'berries' are the dried fruit of the pimento tree, native to the West Indies. Cloves are the dried flower buds of the clove tree, most often associated with baking.

CHICKEN KORMA

| 1.20 | 🍴 | £ £ | ✳ | 408 cals |

Serves 4

50 g (2 oz) blanched almonds

50 g (2 oz) poppy seeds

50 g (2 oz) fresh coconut flesh

4 medium onions, skinned and roughly chopped

2.5-cm (1-inch) piece of fresh root ginger, peeled and roughly chopped

2 garlic cloves, skinned

45 ml (3 tbsp) ghee or 40 g (1½ oz) butter, melted

1.1 kg (2½ lb) chicken, skinned and cut into 8 joints (see page 151)

60 ml (4 tbsp) coarsely chopped coriander leaves

15 ml (1 tbsp) chopped fresh mint leaves or 10 ml (2 tsp) dried mint

30 ml (2 tbsp) ground coriander

2.5 ml (½ tsp) chilli powder

5 ml (1 tsp) salt

45 ml (3 tbsp) lemon juice

120 ml (8 tbsp) natural yogurt

about 450 ml (¾ pint) water

1 Dry-roast the almonds and the poppy seeds in a frying pan or under a grill until the nuts are a pale golden, then transfer to a blender or food processor.

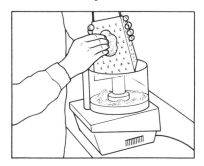

2 Grate the coconut into a blender or processor, then blend to a paste. Remove and set aside.

3 Place the onions, ginger and garlic in the blender or food processor and blend to a paste. Heat the ghee or butter in a large, heavy-based saucepan, add the onion paste and fry until golden, stirring frequently. Add the chicken and fry to a golden colour or until all the moisture in the pan has evaporated.

4 Meanwhile, blend the coriander leaves and mint to a smooth paste. Add all the spices, the salt and the lemon juice and blend together. Add this mixture to the chicken in the pan and fry, stirring frequently, for about 10 minutes so that the chicken is well coated with the spices. Add the coconut mixture and stir in well.

5 Add the yogurt a little at a time to the chicken, stirring continuously to blend it into the mixture. Continue stirring for 3–5 minutes and fry until the ghee begins to separate.

6 Pour in just enough water to cover the chicken, cover the pan, reduce the heat and allow to cook for another 20–30 minutes or until the chicken is really tender. Transfer to a warmed serving dish and serve hot.

Menu Suggestion
Although a mild Indian curry, Chicken Korma is spicily rich. Serve with boiled or pilau rice and the usual accompaniments of chutney, pickle and poppadoms. A spinach curry *(sag bhaji)* also goes well with Chicken Korma.

CHICKEN KORMA
Indian cooking is famed for its korma dishes—chicken or lamb being the most popularly used meats. The meat is simmered in a mixture of pungent spices and herbs which are counterbalanced by the addition of cool, creamy coconut and yogurt—the resultant mixture is irresistibly delicious!

CATALONIAN CHICKEN

| 1.25 | 🍳 | £ £ | ✳ | 446–669 cals |

Serves 4–6

1.4 kg (3 lb) chicken

50 g (2 oz) plus 25 ml (1½ tbsp) flour

salt and freshly ground pepper

50 g (2 oz) butter

45 ml (3 tbsp) vegetable oil

12 button onions, skinned

1 garlic clove, skinned and finely chopped

300 ml (½ pint) chicken stock

30 ml (2 tbsp) white wine (optional)

10 ml (2 tsp) tomato purée

12 chestnuts

225 g (8 oz) chorizo sausages

4 slices of white bread, crusts removed

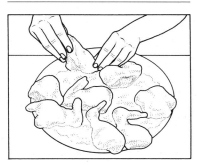

1 Cut the chicken into eight joints and dip in the 100 g (4 oz) flour liberally seasoned with salt and pepper.

2 Heat the butter and 30 ml (2 tbsp) oil in a frying pan, add the chicken joints and fry until well browned. Remove from pan and drain on absorbent kitchen paper.

3 Add the onions and garlic to the pan and fry for 5 minutes until brown, then place in a 1.5–2 litre (3½–4 pint) casserole.

4 Add the remaining flour to the frying pan and stir in the chicken stock, white wine and tomato purée. Bring to a simmer.

5 Place the chicken on top of the onions, and pour the stock over; season. Cover and cook in the oven at 180°C (350°F) mark 4 for 1 hour until tender.

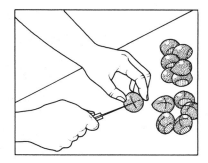

6 To prepare the chestnuts, pierce the brown outer skins with a sharp knife. Plunge into boiling water for 3–5 minutes.

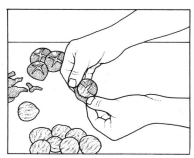

7 Peel off brown and inner skins from the chestnuts. Simmer gently in water for 35 minutes until tender. Fry the sausages, then cut each into three. Add with the chestnuts to the chicken 10 minutes before the end of cooking time.

Menu Suggestion
A plain risotto would make the ideal accompaniment.

CHICKEN MARYLAND

| 0.30 | 679 cals |

Serves 4

1.4 kg (3 lb) chicken, jointed into
   small portions (see page 151)
45 ml (3 tbsp) flour
salt and freshly ground pepper
1 egg, beaten
100 g (4 oz) dried breadcrumbs
50 g (2 oz) butter
15–30 ml (1–2 tbsp) vegetable oil

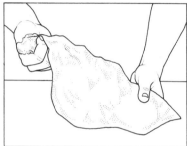

1 Put the chicken portions in a
large polythene bag with the
flour and salt and pepper to taste.
Shake well to coat the chicken in
the flour.

2 Dip the chicken first in the
beaten egg and then roll in the
breadcrumbs to coat.

3 Heat the butter and oil together in a large frying pan,
add the coated chicken and fry for
2–3 minutes until lightly
browned on all sides.

4 Continue frying gently, turning the pieces once, for about
20 minutes, or until tender.
Alternatively, deep-fry the chicken
in hot oil, 170°C (325°F), for 5–10
minutes. Serve the chicken hot
and crisp, with fried bananas and
corn fritters (see above right).

Fried bananas
Peel and slice 4 bananas lengthways. Fry gently in a little hot
butter or chicken fat for about 3
minutes until lightly browned.

Corn fritters
Sift 100 g (4 oz) plain flour and a
pinch of salt into a bowl. Break in
1 egg and add 75 ml (3 fl oz) milk
and beat until smooth. Gradually
beat in a further 75 ml (3 fl oz)
milk. Fold in a 312-g (11-oz) can
sweetcorn kernels, drained. Fry

spoonfuls of the mixture in a little
hot fat for 5 minutes until crisp
and golden, turning once. Drain
well on absorbent kitchen paper.

Menu Suggestion
With its own accompaniments of
fried bananas and corn fritters,
Chicken Maryland needs nothing
further to serve, apart from a crisp
green salad to refresh the palate
afterwards. Ice-cold lager or beer
is the ideal drink to offset the
richness of this dish.

CHICKEN TERIYAKI

| 0.30* | £ | ✳* | 220 cals |

* plus overnight marinating; freeze after step 2

Serves 4

4 boneless chicken breasts, skinned

90 ml (6 tbsp) soy sauce, preferably *shoyu* **(Japanese light soy sauce)**

90 ml (6 tbsp) *sake* **(Japanese rice wine) or dry sherry**

25 g (1 oz) sugar

2 garlic cloves, skinned and crushed

2.5-cm (1-inch) piece of fresh root ginger, peeled and crushed

salt and freshly ground pepper

15–30 ml (1–2 tbsp) vegetable oil

1 Cut the chicken breasts into bite-size pieces. Place the pieces in a shallow bowl.

2 Mix together half the soy sauce, *sake* and sugar, then add half the garlic and ginger with salt and pepper to taste. Pour over the chicken, cover and leave to marinate overnight.

3 Turn the chicken pieces in the marinade occasionally during the marinating time.

4 Thread the cubes of chicken on to oiled kebab skewers. Brush with oil. Barbecue or grill under moderate heat for about 10 minutes until the chicken is tender. Baste the chicken with the marinade and turn frequently during cooking.

5 While the chicken is cooking, put the remaining soy sauce, *sake* and sugar in a small pan with the remaining garlic and ginger. Add salt and pepper to taste and heat through.

6 Serve the chicken hot, with the warmed soy sauce mixture poured over to moisten.

Menu Suggestion
Spicy and sweet, this Japanese skewered chicken looks good on a bed of saffron rice. For an exotic touch, follow with a mixed salad of oriental vegetables such as beansprouts, bamboo shoots, spring onions and fresh root ginger.

CHICKEN TERIYAKI

This is a classic Japanese dish in which pieces of chicken are marinated overnight to tenderise and flavour them, then threaded onto skewers, grilled and served with a hot spicy sauce.

The marinade contains the Japanese rice wine, known as *sake*, which is sold in oriental stores. For a really authentic touch, try using bamboo skewers instead of metal ones—they will need soaking in hot water for about 15 minutes before use.

Pork fillet can be used in place of the chicken.

CIRCASSIAN CHICKEN

1.30	366–549 cals

Serves 4–6

1.8 kg (4 lb) chicken
1 medium onion, skinned and sliced
2 sticks of celery, roughly chopped
1 carrot, peeled and roughly chopped
few sprigs of parsley
salt and freshly ground pepper
100 g (4 oz) shelled walnuts
40 g (1½ oz) butter
45 ml (3 tbsp) vegetable oil
1.25 ml (¼ tsp) ground cinnamon
1.25 ml (¼ tsp) ground cloves
5 ml (1 tsp) paprika

1 Put the chicken in a large saucepan with the vegetables, parsley, 5 ml (1 tsp) salt and pepper to taste. Cover the chicken with water and bring to the boil. Lower heat, half cover pan with a lid and simmer for 40 minutes.

2 Remove the chicken from the pan, strain the cooking liquid and set aside. Cut the chicken into serving pieces, discarding the skin.

3 Pound the walnuts with a pestle in a mortar until very fine, or grind them in an electric grinder or food processor.

4 Melt the butter with 15 ml (1 tbsp) oil in a large frying pan. Add the chicken pieces and fry over moderate heat for 3–4 minutes until well coloured.

5 Add 450 ml (¾ pint) of the cooking liquid, the walnuts, cinnamon and cloves. Stir well to mix, then simmer uncovered for about 20 minutes or until the chicken is tender and the sauce thickly coats the chicken. Stir the chicken and sauce frequently during this time.

6 Just before serving, heat the remaining oil in a separate small pan. Sprinkle in the paprika, stirring to combine with the oil.

7 Taste and adjust the seasoning of the walnut sauce. Arrange the chicken and sauce on a warmed serving platter and drizzle with the paprika oil. Serve at once.

Menu Suggestion
For a Middle-Eastern style meal, serve the chicken and walnut sauce in a ring of saffron rice. Follow with a tomato, onion and black olive salad sprinkled with olive oil and lemon juice.

TURKEY MOLE

0.30	483 cals

Serves 4

50 g (2 oz) butter

15 ml (1 tbsp) vegetable oil

4 turkey escalopes

salt and freshly ground pepper

450 ml ($\frac{3}{4}$ pint) chicken stock

1 green pepper, cored, seeded and chopped

2.5 ml ($\frac{1}{2}$ tsp) aniseed

15 ml (1 tbsp) sesame seeds

2 garlic cloves, skinned and crushed

pinch of ground cloves

pinch of ground cinnamon

1.25 ml ($\frac{1}{4}$ tsp) coriander seeds

50 g (2 oz) plain chocolate, grated

45 ml (3 tbsp) ground almonds

2.5 ml ($\frac{1}{2}$ tsp) chilli powder

3 tomatoes, skinned

1 Heat the butter and oil in a frying pan and fry the turkey escalopes for 2–3 minutes until brown on all sides. Drain on absorbent kitchen paper and place in an ovenproof casserole.

2 Place all the remaining ingredients in a blender or food processor and purée until smooth.

3 Pour the blended sauce over the turkey and cover. Bake in the oven at 180°C (350°F) mark 4 for 20 minutes until the turkey is tender.

Menu Suggestion
With its rich and flavoursome sauce, Turkey Mole from Mexico needs only a green salad as an accompaniment.

TRADITIONAL ROAST CHICKEN

(illustrated on cover)

2.00	351–526 cals

Serves 4–6

1.8–2.3 kg (4–5 lb) chicken

sage and onion stuffing (see page 155)

1 medium onion, skinned

½ lemon

50 g (2 oz) butter

salt and freshly ground pepper

4 streaky bacon rashers

1 If the chicken is frozen, allow it to thaw out completely. A 1.8-kg (4-lb) bird will take 8–10 hours at room temperature.

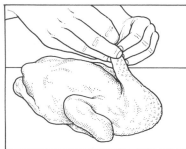

2 Wash the bird and dry thoroughly. Spoon the stuffing into the neck end, then fold over the neck skin. To add flavour, put the onion and lemon in the body of the bird.

3 Weigh the chicken and place it in a deep roasting tin. Spread with the butter and sprinkle with salt and pepper.

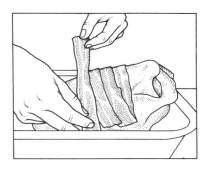

4 Place the streaky bacon rashers over the breast of the bird, to prevent it from becoming dry.

5 Roast in the oven at 200°C (400°F) mark 6, basting from time to time, and allowing 20 minutes per 450 g (1 lb) plus 20 minutes extra.

6 Put a piece of foil over the breast if it shows signs of becoming too brown. The chicken is cooked if the juices run clear when the thickest part of the leg is pierced with a knife or skewer.

Menu Suggestion
The traditional accompaniments to sage-and-onion-stuffed roast chicken in England are roast and creamed potatoes and fresh vegetables such as Brussels sprouts and carrots. Bread sauce and giblet gravy are also traditional, as are chipolata sausages and bacon rolls which have been cooked around the chicken.

TRADITIONAL ROAST CHICKEN

No roast is complete without a well-flavoured gravy to accompany it. You can either make a giblet gravy (see page 157) as suggested above, or for a change make a gravy or 'jus' in the French style, adding a little wine to enhance the flavour of the chicken.

To make this gravy pour off as much fat from the roasting tin as possible. Place the tin over the heat on top of the stove and let the sediment bubble up for a few minutes, stirring until nicely coloured. Add about **300 ml (½ pint) home-made chicken stock** or vegetable cooking water and a dash of **red or white wine**. Boil rapidly, stirring occasionally to mix well, until reduced by almost half. Season and strain.

PEKING DUCK WITH THIN PANCAKES

4.00* ⊟ ⊟ £ £ 768 cals

* plus chilling during the previous day and overnight

Serves 4

2.3 kg (5 lb) duck
4.5 litres (8 pints) boiling water
15 ml (1 tbsp) salt
15 ml (1 tbsp) dry sherry
thin pancakes (see below)
60 ml (4 tbsp) maple-flavoured syrup
100 ml (4 fl oz) hoisin sauce
4 spring onions, cut into 5-cm (2-inch) pieces

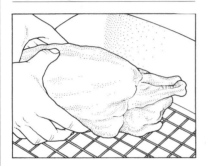

1 Early on the day before serving the duck, rinse the bird and drain on a rack in the sink. Pour the boiling water slowly over the duck until the skin whitens. Drain well.

2 Gently pat dry the skin and body cavity with absorbent kitchen paper. Rub the body cavity with the salt and sherry.

3 Put the duck, breast side down, on a rack in a roasting tin and refrigerate until the evening. Do not cover. Meanwhile, make the thin pancakes.

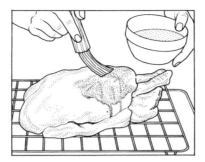

4 Early that evening, brush the duck all over with maple syrup. Leave on rack, breast side up, and refrigerate uncovered overnight.

5 About 3 hours before serving, put the duck breast down on its rack in the tin, and cook in the oven at 190°C (375°F) mark 5 for 1½ hours. Turn, and cook for 1–1½ hours more until the skin is crisp and golden.

6 To serve, slice the duck thinly into pieces about 5 × 2.5 cm (2 × 1 inch) and arrange on a warmed plate. Put the hoisin sauce in a small bowl and the spring onions on a small plate.

7 Each person assembles their own portion. Put one or two slices of duck in the centre of a pancake, add a dab of hoisin sauce and some spring onion. Roll up, and eat with your hands.

THIN PANCAKES

275 g (10 oz) flour
2.5 ml (½ tsp) salt
225 g (8 fl oz) boiling water
vegetable oil, for brushing

1 Sift the flour and salt into a large bowl. Gradually blend in the boiling water with a fork.

2 Press the dough into a ball, place on a floured surface and knead for about 5 minutes.

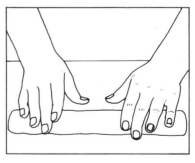

3 Shape the dough into a roll measuring about 40 cm (16 inches) long.

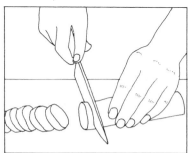

4 Slice crossways into sixteen pieces. Cover with a damp cloth. Take two pieces of dough at a time and put them on a lightly floured surface.

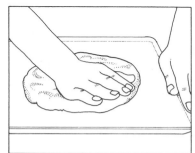

5 Flatten into 10 cm (4-inch) circles. Brush with oil. Place the circles one on top of another, oiled surfaces together. With a lightly floured rolling pin, roll from the centre to form a 20-cm (8-inch) circle.

6 Heat an ungreased frying pan. Add the circle of dough and cook each side for 2–3 minutes or until light brown. Remove to an ovenproof plate and separate the two layers. Stack the pancakes, browned side up, and cover with foil. Repeat to make 16 pancakes.

7 To reheat, put the plate of pancakes over a pan of boiling water and cover with foil. Reduce the heat and simmer until hot.

Menu Suggestion
Serve as part of a Chinese feast — after a first course of soup or pancake rolls and before a stir-fried main course.

CASSOULET

3.30 ☐ £ £ 508 cals
Serves 12

700 g (1½ lb) dried white haricot
  beans

225 g (8 oz) salt pork or bacon, in
  one piece

450 g (1 lb) loin or shoulder of pork,
  boned

30 ml (2 tbsp) vegetable oil or fat
  from preserved goose

2 medium onions, skinned and
  thinly sliced

3 garlic cloves, skinned and finely
  chopped

1.4 kg (3 lb) shoulder of lamb
  (or ½ large shoulder), boned

1 piece of preserved goose

450 g (1 lb) piece coarse pork and
  garlic sausage

60 ml (4 tbsp) tomato purée

1.7 litres (3 pints) water

salt and freshly ground pepper

1 bouquet garni

100 g (4 oz) fresh breadcrumbs (see
  step 8 of method)

1 Rinse the beans in cold water, then put into a large saucepan. Cover with cold water, bring slowly to the boil and simmer for 5 minutes. Remove from the heat, cover and leave to soak in the water while you prepare the remaining ingredients.

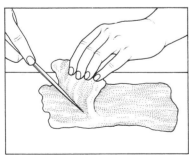

2 Remove the rind from the salt pork or bacon, and from the pork, and cut it into small squares.

3 Heat the oil or goose fat in a large frying pan and fry the onions and garlic for 5 minutes until softened. Add the pieces of pork rind and fry gently for 5 minutes. Raise the heat and brown on all sides, in turn, the pork and salt pork, the shoulder of lamb, the piece of goose and the sausage. Remove each from the pan when it is browned and set aside.

4 Add the tomato purée to the pan with a little of the water, stir well to amalgamate any sediment and bring quickly to the boil.

5 Drain the beans, rinse them and put them in a clean saucepan with the remaining cold water. Bring to the boil, then pour the beans and water into a cassoulet pot or large flameproof casserole.

6 Add the contents of the frying pan, salt and pepper to taste and stir well. Bury the salt pork or bacon, the pork, the shoulder of lamb, the preserved goose and the sausage among the beans, add the bouquet garni, and bring to simmering point on top of the stove.

7 Sprinkle on a thick layer of breadcrumbs. Cook in the oven at 150°C (300°F) mark 2 for 2–3 hours, until the meat and beans are tender.

8 From time to time press down the crust which will have formed on top and sprinkle on a further layer of breadcrumbs. Tradition has it that the crust must be pressed down and renewed seven times, but three times should give an attractive golden crust. Cut up larger pieces of meat before serving.

Menu Suggestion
In France, Cassoulet is served on its own, with only chunks of fresh *baguette* (French stick) to accompany it. Follow with a crisp green salad tossed in a sharp vinaigrette dressing for a very filling meal.

CASSOULET
Cassoulet is a hearty peasant dish which originates from the Languedoc region of southern France. There are, of course, many different variations, but the central theme is a casserole of haricot beans, flavoured with tomato and cooked for several hours with a mixture of fresh and preserved meats and poultry until they are all completely tender and the flavoursome juices amalgamated. A breadcrumb topping acts as a seal on top, conserving all the goodness in the casserole and acting as a deliciously crunchy contrast to the meat and beans below.

Preserved goose, a traditional ingredient of cassoulet, is available canned from most good grocers.

CHRISTMAS ROAST GOOSE

| 2.35 | 🍴 | £ £ | 744 cals |

Serves 6

3.2–3.6 kg (7–8 lb) goose

½ lemon

salt and freshly ground pepper

350 g (12 oz) cooking apples, cored and roughly chopped

450 g (1 lb) prunes, soaked, stoned and chopped

25 g (1 oz) butter or margarine

40 g (1½ oz) flour

60 ml (4 tbsp) redcurrant jelly (optional)

For the garnish

175 g (6 oz) sugar

300 ml (½ pint) water

4 even-sized eating apples, peeled, cored and halved

225 g (8 oz) prunes

port, sherry or Madeira

whole blanched almonds (optional)

1 Remove the neck, giblets and fat from the body cavity and reserve the neck and giblets for making the gravy.

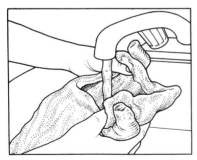

2 Rinse the goose under cold running water (letting the water run through the body cavity). Dry inside and out with absorbent kitchen paper.

3 Rub the cavity inside and out with the lemon and season with salt and pepper. Mix together the chopped apples and prunes and stuff the cavity.

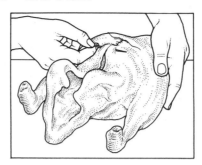

4 Sew or skewer the opening, to contain the stuffing, then weigh the bird.

5 Prick the bird all over with a sharp skewer or fork to let the fat run during cooking. Rub the skin with salt, and place the bird on a trivet or rack in a roasting tin containing 1 cm (½ inch) water. Place the neck and giblets (except the liver) in the water.

6 Roast in the oven at 220°C (425°F) mark 7 for 20 minutes. Cover the breast with greased paper and reduce the heat to 180°C (350°F) mark 4 and roast for 13–15 minutes per 450 g (1 lb). About 20 minutes before the end of the cooking time, uncover the breast and pour off the liquid from the tin. Reserve for gravy.

7 Meanwhile, prepare the garnish. In a shallow pan, dissolve 125 g (4 oz) of the sugar in the water. Boil for 3 minutes, then lower the heat to a gentle simmer. Add the apple halves and simmer for about 10–15 minutes until just tender. Lift out the apples with a slotted spoon and keep warm.

8 In a different saucepan, cover the prunes with water and bring to the boil. Drain, return the prunes to the pan and add the remaining 50 g (2 oz) sugar and enough port, sherry or madeira to cover the prunes. Simmer for 15–20 minutes. Cool for 15 minutes then drain, reserving the wine.

9 Remove the stones from the prunes carefully and, if liked, replace each stone with a blanched almond. Place a prune in each apple hollow and keep warm.

10 Skim the fat off the reserved roasting juices and strain the liquid to remove the neck and giblets. Add enough water to make up to 450 ml (¾ pint) and transfer to a saucepan. Bring to the boil. Cream together the fat and flour and gradually whisk into the liquid. As the butter melts, the gravy will thicken.

11 Simmer for 5 minutes and finally stir in the redcurrant jelly (if using) with the reserved wine. Simmer again for 5 minutes and check seasoning, adding more water if gravy is too thick.

12 Serve the goose surrounded by the stuffed apple halves and hand the gravy separately.

Menu Suggestion

Serve with roast potatoes and Brussels sprouts. A beetroot salad with horseradish dressing would offset the richness of the goose.

POLLO CACCIATORA

| 0.50 | £ ✳ | 458 cals |

Serves 4

25 g (1 oz) butter

30 ml (2 tbsp) olive oil

4 chicken portions

1 medium onion, skinned and chopped

2 garlic cloves, skinned and crushed

225 g (8 oz) button mushrooms, sliced

150 ml ($\frac{1}{4}$ pint) dry white wine

397-g (14-oz) can tomatoes, drained

10 ml (2 tsp) dried mixed herbs

5 ml (1 tsp) dried oregano

salt and freshly ground pepper

1 Melt the butter with the oil in a large flameproof casserole. Add the chicken and fry over moderate heat for 5–10 minutes until well coloured on all sides. Remove from the pan with a slotted spoon and drain on absorbent kitchen paper.

2 Add the onion and garlic to the pan and fry gently until soft. Return the chicken to the pan, add the mushrooms and wine and simmer for 10 minutes.

3 Add the tomatoes, herbs and salt and pepper to taste, then cover and simmer for a further 35 minutes or until the chicken is tender. Taste and adjust seasoning before serving.

Menu Suggestion
In Italy, Pollo Cacciatora is traditionally served with *polenta*, a simple dish of cornmeal. Place a chicken portion and some *polenta* on each individual dinner plate, then pour the sauce from the chicken over the *polenta*.

USEFUL INFORMATION
AND
BASIC RECIPES

Cooking Poultry

It is the versatility of poultry which makes it such a favourite with both the cook and her family and friends. Each of the basic cooking methods can be used — choose your recipe depending on the type, size and age of the bird and on whether you are cooking joints or a whole bird.

GRILLING

Grilling is a quick method of cooking, searing the meat with a dry heat. It is therefore suitable only for the tenderest meats. Portions of young chicken such as poussins, spring chickens or small roasting birds are ideal. The outside will be crisp and brown, the inside moist and juicy.

Whole birds are not suitable for grilling and large portions on the bone, such as turkey legs, are too uneven to grill well. But boneless steaks of light or dark turkey meat grill well and the boneless meat can also be cut into chunks for kebabs. Grilled duck breasts are good but don't grill the legs as they tend to burn on the outside before they are cooked through to the bone. For a special occasion, grill a spatchcocked guinea fowl.

To prevent the meat from drying in the heat of the grill, brush it well with melted butter or oil before and during cooking, or marinate it first to add extra juiciness and flavour.

Always preheat the grill to give the skin a good crisp outside and cook under a steady, moderate heat. Try to select portions of a similar thickness—chicken legs for example take longer to cook than the breast portions, so add breasts to the grill pan about 5 minutes after the legs.

Poultry must be cooked through to the bone, so pierce the thickest part of the flesh with a skewer to check. The meat is cooked when the juices run clear.

BARBECUING
When grilling on a barbecue, be sure to light the fire well ahead. It will take at least 30 minutes for the charcoal to reach the correct heat for cooking; there should be no flames or red coals but the heat should be steady and even.

There is a tendency for poultry to cook too fast over charcoal; if this happens, raise the grid further from the fire or move the centre portions to the outside of the grid,

Wrapping meat in foil

which will be cooler. If necessary, brown the outside then continue cooking wrapped in foil.

TURKEY AND SAUSAGE KEBABS
Serves 6

1.1–1.4 kg (2½–3 lb) turkey meat
75 ml (5 tbsp) soy sauce
75 ml (5 tbsp) dry sherry
15 ml (1 tbsp) sugar
45 ml (3 tbsp) vegetable oil
225 g (8 oz) sausages
8 large spring onions, trimmed
226-g (8-oz) can pineapple, drained

1 Cut the turkey into 2.5-cm (1-inch) chunks. Mix the soy sauce, sherry, sugar and oil.

2 Add the turkey pieces and coat with the marinade. Cover and refrigerate for 30 minutes.

3 Meanwhile, halve the sausages crossways and cut the spring onions into 4-cm (1½-inch) pieces.

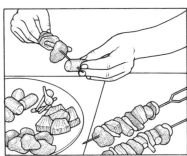

4 Thread chunks of turkey, sausage, pineapple and spring onion alternately on to skewers.

5 Cook under a hot grill for 20–25 minutes until the meat is tender, turning the kebabs and basting with the marinade.

TANDOORI CHICKEN

Serves 8

8 chicken joints

salt and freshly ground pepper

lemon wedges and chopped fresh coriander leaves, to garnish

For the marinade

225 ml (8 fl oz) natural yogurt

5 ml (1 tsp) freshly ground pepper

10 ml (2 tsp) salt

7.5 ml (1½ tsp) chilli powder

pinch of ground ginger

pinch of ground coriander

1 large garlic clove, skinned and crushed

juice of 1½ lemons

1 Wipe the chicken joints, prick skin with a fork and season. Combine the yogurt with all of the remaining marinade ingredients.

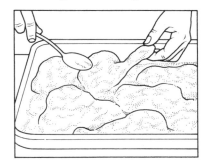

2 Add the chicken pieces, turning to coat well. Cover and leave to stand for 3–4 hours, turning occasionally.

3 Place the chicken, skin side down, in a grill pan and baste with some of the marinade. Grill for 25 minutes under medium heat; turn and baste again. Grill for a further 15 minutes or until the chicken is tender.

4 Transfer the chicken to a heated serving dish and garnish with lemon and coriander.

SAVOURY CHICKEN

Serves 4

1.4–1.6 kg (3–3½ lb) chicken, quartered

For the marinade

10 medium garlic cloves, skinned

175 ml (6 fl oz) tarragon vinegar

25 g (1 oz) sugar

15 ml (1 tbsp) vegetable oil

15 ml (1 tbsp) Worcestershire sauce

10 ml (2 tsp) mustard powder

5 ml (1 tsp) salt

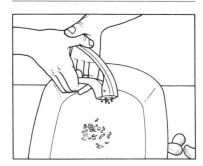

1 Crush the garlic cloves and put into a large, shallow dish. Add the remaining ingredients for the marinade and mix well.

2 Prick the skin of the chicken pieces with a fork and add to marinade, turning to coat. Cover and refrigerate for at least 2 hours.

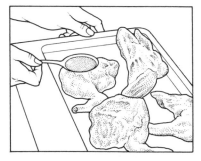

3 Place the chicken, skin side down, in a grill pan and baste with the marinade. Grill under medium heat for 40 minutes, or until the chicken is tender, turning once and basting with the marinade during cooking.

─────── VARIATION ───────

BARBECUED CHICKEN

Marinate the chicken as above. Prepare an outdoor grill; pour a little melted butter on each chicken joint and place on the barbecue grid over very hot coals. Brown quickly on all sides then remove from the grid and place each joint on a 38-cm (15-inch) square piece of foil. Wrap round the chicken and seal the edges securely. Place each packet on the grid and cook for a further 20 minutes, turning once. Heat the marinade in a small saucepan and serve separately as a sauce. Serve

the chicken in the foil packets so that none of the buttery juices are lost.

GRILLED DUCK BREASTS

Serves 4

4 duck breasts, with skin on

salt

For the marinade

200 ml (7 fl oz) vegetable oil

100 ml (4 fl oz) red wine

5 ml (1 tsp) salt

freshly ground pepper

1 large onion, skinned and thinly sliced

3 large garlic cloves, skinned and thinly sliced

2 bay leaves, roughly crumbled

1 In a shallow dish large enough to hold the duck breasts in one layer, mix all the marinade ingredients together.

2 Lay the duck breasts in the marinade, baste thoroughly, cover, and marinate for at least 3 hours, turning the pieces from time to time.

3 Remove the breasts from the marinade. Strain the marinade through a fine sieve and discard the flavourings.

4 Arrange the duck breasts, skin side down, on the grill rack, sprinkle lightly with salt and grill 10 cm (4 inches) from high heat for about 15 minutes, lowering the heat or the rack so that the duck browns slowly without burning. Baste every 5 minutes or so with the strained marinade.

5 Turn the breasts over, sprinkle with salt again, and grill for a further 10–15 minutes, basting two or three times with the strained marinade.

6 When the duck is tender and a deep golden-brown, arrange the pieces on a heated serving dish, and serve immediately.

POUSSINS IN A BASKET

Serves 4

4 poussins

100 g (4 oz) butter or margarine, melted

salt and freshly ground pepper

2 medium onions, skinned and sliced, and watercress, to garnish

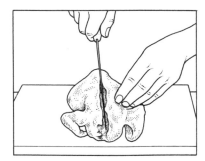

1 With a heavy knife, split the poussins down the back. Trim off the legs and the wings at the first joints, open out the birds and flatten them as much as possible. Run a long skewer through from leg to leg on each bird to hold flat.

2 Brush each bird all over with melted fat and season lightly. Grill under medium heat for about 20 minutes, turning the birds once or twice, or until the poussins are cooked through and are tender.

3 Serve each bird on a napkin in a basket, garnished with onion rings and sprigs of watercress.

SPIT ROASTING

Spit roasting achieves a similar effect to grilling for whole birds or large joints. Many gas and electric cookers can be fitted with a rotisserie for the purpose, or you can buy a separate, electrically operated model. A charcoal barbecue may be fitted with a battery-operated spit.

For the best results choose a small bird, up to about 1.6 kg ($3\frac{1}{2}$ lb). Remove the giblets and rinse and dry the bird inside and out. Fold the neck skin over the

back and skewer it in position. Tie the wings close to the body. Insert

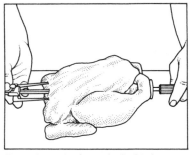

Inserting spit through the bird

the spit through the body from end to end and tighten the holding prongs. Make sure the bird is balanced on the spit.

Using fine string, tie the parson's nose and drumsticks securely on to the spit. Check that the spit will revolve freely and evenly.

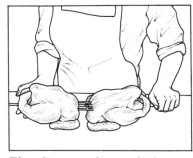

Threading more than one bird

If you are cooking more than one bird at a time, thread them on to the spit in opposite directions to make sure they balance properly.

Preheat the grill, barbecue or rotisserie and place the loaded spit in position. Place a drip tray under the bird to catch the melting fat, and use the fat to baste the bird occasionally as it cooks. Cook for about $1\frac{1}{2}$ hours. If you are using a basting sauce, use it only during the last 20 minutes or so of cooking time.

MARINATING

A marinade is a convenient, trouble-free way of flavouring and tenderising poultry. It is ideal to use in conjunction with quick cooking methods like grilling and barbecuing. Soak the poultry for a few hours beforehand in the flavoursome liquid, then use any remaining marinade in a sauce.

A marinade is generally based on a fat or oil to give dry meat extra moisture. Olive oil is a good choice, but other more or less highly flavoured oils are also suitable. A liquid such as yogurt will serve the same purpose for a special recipe. As well as the oil you need an acid ingredient to break down the fibres in the meat—wine, vinegar or lemon juice are the usual choices for this. Add spices or herbs for flavour.

Vary a basic marinade and add extra zing by using bottled relishes. These frequently contain vinegar as the preservative and the blend of spices included will save you making up your own recipe.

For marinating you can use fresh or frozen poultry—this is an excellent way of adding flavour to a factory-bred bird. But thaw a frozen bird completely and dry it well before you put it in the marinade, or the liquid will be diluted with water from the bird.

To marinate a whole bird, put the flavouring liquid in a large polythene bag, add the bird and place it in a deep dish. Turn the

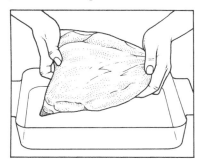

Soaking the whole of the bird

bag and bird from time to time to soak the whole of the bird.

For poultry portions, choose a large shallow dish that will take all the pieces in a single layer; don't use an aluminium or enamelled iron pan as these could be damaged by the acid. Mix the marinade ingredients thoroughly.

Dry the poultry well on absorbent kitchen paper and prick the skin all over with a fork, to help the flavour penetrate. Place the pieces in the dish in a single layer and spoon or brush the liquid all over them. Cover with

Covering with cling film

cling film and leave for at least 2 hours, turning the pieces occasionally. If the room is warm or if you are leaving it for longer than 2 hours, place the dish in the refrigerator until required.

When you are ready to cook, drain the marinade off each portion but save the remaining liquid for basting during cooking and for making a sauce to serve with the finished dish.

SPRING ONION AND SOY MARINADE

100 ml (4 fl oz) soy sauce	
30 ml (2 tbsp) dry sherry	
50 g (2 oz) spring onions, thinly sliced	
30 ml (2 tbsp) soft light brown sugar	
2.5 ml ($\frac{1}{2}$ tsp) salt	
2.5 ml ($\frac{1}{2}$ tsp) ground ginger	

Mix the ingredients in a shallow dish and blend well. Spoon over the chicken and marinate for at least 2 hours.

CHICKEN WITH CHILLI MARINADE

Serves 4

1.4 kg (3 lb) chicken, quartered or jointed

For the marinade

350-g (12-oz) bottle mild chilli relish
5 ml (1 tsp) salt
10 ml (2 tsp) dried horseradish
1 garlic clove, skinned and quartered
100 ml (4 fl oz) wine vinegar

1 Prick the chicken skin all over with a fork. Mix all the marinade ingredients in a large dish. Add the chicken pieces and coat well. Cover and refrigerate for at least 2 hours, turning from time to time.

2 Arrange the chicken in a single layer in the grill pan. Grill for 35–45 minutes under medium heat, until tender, turning frequently and basting with the chilli marinade.

ORANGE HERB MARINADE

150 ml ($\frac{1}{4}$ pint) white wine or dry vermouth
45 ml (3 tbsp) olive oil
juice of 2 oranges
5 ml (1 tsp) each chopped fresh rosemary, thyme and marjoram
1 garlic clove, skinned and crushed

Mix the ingredients in a shallow dish and stir until well blended. Spoon over the chicken and marinate for at least 2 hours.

LIME MARINADE

100 ml (4 fl oz) lime juice
45 ml (3 tbsp) vegetable oil
15 ml (1 tbsp) grated lime rind
20 ml (4 tsp) salt
1.25 ml ($\frac{1}{4}$ tsp) crushed peppercorns

Mix the ingredients in a shallow dish and stir until well blended. Spoon over the chicken and marinate for at least 2 hours.

PAN FRYING AND SAUTÉS

Individual portions of poultry are ideal for frying and sautés. The secret is to sear the surface quickly first, to seal in the juices and give a good brown colour, then reduce the heat and cook slowly until the meat is cooked right through and tender.

Drying meat well

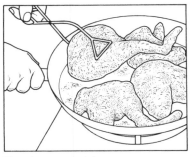

Turning meat with tongs

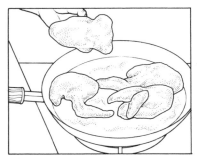

Frying poultry in single layer

When frying poultry, choose a wide, heavy-based, shallow pan that will take the pieces in a single layer; or use two pans. If you layer one piece on top of another they will stew rather than fry. For sautés in which the cooking is finished in a sauce you will need a tightly fitting lid, or a sheet of foil.

Choose oil, butter, margarine or rendered chicken fat for frying. In many dishes, particularly those finished with a delicate or creamy sauce, butter gives the best flavour. Use clarified butter if possible as the high temperature can cause ordinary butter to burn, leaving black specks on the meat and spoiling the flavour. Or use part oil and part butter, which will help prevent the butter burning. Oil alone will give you a good crisp outside, with less flavour but also with less risk of burning.

If the poultry is to be cooked without a coating, it must be completely dry when it goes into the hot fat. A coating of flour or breadcrumbs will help contain the juices and prevent the outer meat from hardening in the hot fat.

If using flour alone, dry the meat well and roll it in seasoned flour just before cooking; if left to stand after coating, the flour will turn to paste with the moisture from the meat.

If coating with breadcrumbs, on the other hand, it is best to chill the coated pieces briefly before cooking to help the coating adhere. Roll the portions in flour first to absorb any moisture, then dip in beaten egg and roll in

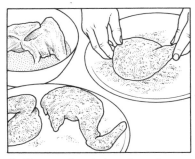

Rolling portions in breadcrumbs

breadcrumbs. Pat the crumbs on firmly and chill for about 15 minutes for the best results. The moisture will be absorbed by the flour and will not soak through to the crumbs.

To cook, heat the fat to frying temperature and add the poultry pieces in a single layer. Remember that the side that goes into the fat first will look the best, so portions with bone should go in fleshy side down. Cook briskly until golden,

then turn the meat with tongs or two spoons to avoid piercing the flesh. Cook until the second side is golden then reduce the heat, cover the pan if the recipe calls for it, and continue cooking until the meat is tender and cooked.

Depending on the recipe you can then either add a little liquid to the poultry in the pan and make a small amount of sauce, or remove the cooked poultry to keep hot while you make a sauce.

STIR-FRIED POULTRY

Stir-frying is the traditional Chinese way of cooking high-quality meats. Very thin slices of

Stir-frying thinly sliced meat

meat are cooked and stirred over high heat in a small amount of oil. Cooking is very quick and the result should be crisp and tender. Fine-fleshed, lean poultry is an ideal meat for stir-fried dishes.

Stir-fried recipes invariably include a variety of vegetables, which serve both to extend a small quantity of poultry and to give the blend of many flavours that is typical of Chinese foods.

FRIED CHICKEN WITH PARSLEY SAUCE

Serves 4

1.1–1.4 kg (2½–3 lb) chicken, jointed
salt and freshly ground pepper
flour
vegetable oil
For the sauce
15 ml (1 tbsp) flour
150 ml (¼ pint) milk
150 ml (¼ pint) chicken stock
salt and freshly ground pepper
15–30 ml (1–2 tbsp) chopped
    parsley

1 Season the chicken pieces with salt and pepper and roll them in the flour to completely coat.

2 Using a large frying pan, pour in enough oil to cover the bottom of the pan. Heat the oil and fry the chicken, turning the pieces, until brown.

3 Reduce the heat and cook the chicken for 15 minutes on each side until tender. Remove from the pan with kitchen tongs, arrange the chicken pieces on a warmed serving dish and keep hot.

4 Drain off all but 30 ml (2 tbsp) oil and sprinkle in 15 ml (1 tbsp) flour. Cook over medium heat, stirring until well browned.

5 Blend in the liquids. Bring the sauce to the boil, stirring all the time, and boil for 2–3 minutes or until thickened. Adjust the seasoning, then add the parsley and pour sauce over the chicken.

CURRIED TURKEY WITH AVOCADO

Serves 4

350 g (12 oz) turkey fillet
30 ml (2 tbsp) flour
15 ml (1 tbsp) ground cumin
15 ml (1 tbsp) ground ginger
salt and freshly ground pepper
1 egg, beaten
1 ripe but still firm avocado
15 ml (1 tbsp) lemon juice
about 45 ml (3 tbsp) peanut oil
1 garlic clove, crushed
225-g (8-oz) can bamboo shoots,
    drained and thinly sliced
1 bunch spring onions, chopped

1 Slice the turkey into strips. Toss in the flour, cumin, ginger and seasonings. Stir in the egg.

2 Peel and slice the avocado. Coat in lemon juice.

3 Heat the oil, with the garlic, in a large frying pan. Add the turkey strips, fry over a high heat, stirring all the time, until golden, adding more oil if necessary.

4 Reduce heat, stir in the bamboo shoots and spring onions. Cook, stirring, for 1–2 minutes. Off heat fold in avocado.

CHINESE CHICKEN WITH VEGETABLES

Serves 4

450 g (1 lb) chicken meat
45 ml (3 tbsp) vegetable oil
5 ml (1 tsp) salt
30 ml (2 tbsp) soy sauce
2–3 sticks of celery, trimmed
½ green pepper, seeded
270-g (9½-oz) can beansprouts
100-g (4-oz) can water chestnuts
50 g (2 oz) mushrooms
150 ml (¼ pint) chicken stock
15 ml (1 tbsp) cornflour
salt and freshly ground pepper
50 g (2 oz) flaked almonds, toasted

1 Carefully slice the uncooked chicken into thin strips, about 0.5 cm (¼ inch) wide.

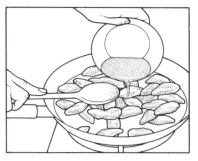

2 Heat the oil in a large frying pan and add the chicken and salt. Stir-fry for 3–5 minutes. Add the soy sauce and blend well.

3 Slice the celery and green pepper into thin strips. Add with the drained beansprouts and chestnuts, mushrooms and stock. Cover and simmer for 15 minutes.

4 Blend the cornflour with a little water and add to the pan. Bring slowly to the boil, stirring. Season and sprinkle with almonds.

SAUTÉ OF DUCKLING WITH PEAS

Serves 4

1.8 kg (4 lb) duckling, jointed
15 ml (1 tbsp) flour
300 ml (½ pint) jellied chicken stock
150 ml (¼ pint) red wine
15 ml (1 tbsp) fresh chopped sage
salt and freshly ground pepper
450 g (1 lb) fresh peas, podded

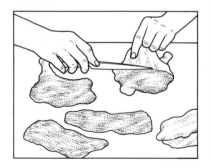

1 Ease the skin and fat off the duckling joints and halve the leg joints. Snip the skin into small pieces and brown in a large sauté pan until crisp. Set aside.

2 Drain off all but 45 ml (3 tbsp) fat from the sauté pan and brown the duckling joints. Sprinkle in the flour, stir to combine with the fat and cook gently for 1 minute. Stir in the stock, wine, sage and seasoning and bring to the boil. Cover the pan and simmer for 25 minutes, then turn the duckling pieces over.

3 Add the peas to the sauté pan, submerging them as far as possible. Cover and continue simmering for 25 minutes, or until duckling and peas are tender.

4 Adjust the seasoning and garnish with the reserved pieces of crisp duck skin.

LEMON SESAME CHICKEN

Serves 4

8 small chicken drumsticks, about 75 g (3 oz) each
30 ml (2 tbsp) cornflour
1 egg, beaten
225 g (8 oz) leeks, trimmed
1 lemon
15 ml (1 tbsp) soy sauce
15 ml (1 tbsp) cider vinegar
15 ml (1 tbsp) demerara sugar
60 ml (4 tbsp) dry sherry
about 15 ml (1 tbsp) sesame oil
about 30 ml (2 tbsp) peanut oil
salt and freshly ground pepper

1 Cover the drumsticks with cold water and bring to the boil. Simmer for about 30 minutes until tender. Drain and pat dry with absorbent kitchen paper.

2 Mix together the cornflour and egg; use to thoroughly coat the chicken drumsticks.

3 Cut the leeks into 1-cm (½-inch) slices. Grate the rind from the lemon. Whisk together the grated lemon rind, soy sauce, cider vinegar, sugar and sherry.

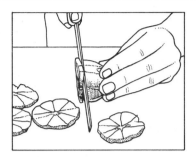

4 Peel and thinly slice the lemon. Heat the oils together in a wok or large frying pan until smoky hot. Brown the drumsticks a few at a time. Remove.

5 Over a medium heat, fry the leeks and sesame seeds for 1–2 minutes, adding more oil if necessary. Return all the drumsticks with the sauce mixture to the pan. Raise heat, bring to the boil and simmer for 3–4 minutes, stirring occasionally. Season.

6 Transfer to a warmed serving dish. Lightly sauté the lemon slices in the wok or frying pan. Garnish the drumsticks with the lemon and serve immediately.

ROASTING POULTRY

Roast poultry is the traditional dinner for Christmas and many other celebrations. It is also popular as an alternative to a roast joint for Sunday lunch. The presentation of the bird may be as elaborate or simple as you like, but the technique remains the same.

Roasting was originally a method of cooking by the fierce dry heat in front of an open fire. The term is now used almost universally to mean 'oven-roasting', or baking. The heat is still fierce but the confines of the oven keep the air moist and the flesh of the bird retains its juices.

Good roast poultry has a well-browned, crisp and tasty skin without losing the succulence of the flesh beneath. Achieving this is perhaps easiest with a chicken. This smallish bird has a fairly even distribution of flesh and fat over the bones and will cook evenly with a minimum of effort.

A duck is more difficult. The skin is very fatty indeed and it is a skilled job to crisp the skin without cooking the inner flesh to a frazzle. A goose gives similar problems, compounded by the larger size of the bird. With both these birds, prick the skin all over with a fork before you start to cook, to allow the fat to run out freely. Then stand the bird on a

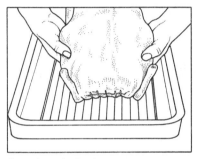

Standing the bird on a rack

rack in the roasting tin, clear of the fat which collects. Very little basting is required. A turkey is lean by comparison but there is a marked contrast in textures between the light meat of the breast and the dark meat of legs and wings; the difficulty with turkey is to cook the dark meat sufficiently without overcooking the breast.

Covering the bird with foil protects the breast, but you must remember to remove it 30 minutes before the end of cooking to allow the skin to brown. It also helps if you start the bird cooking breast side down, turning it the 'right way up' after the dark meat is partially cooked.

Guinea fowl is generally smaller than chicken and has very little fat. Take care, therefore, to add plenty of extra fat while cooking, to baste well and never overcook. A quail is equally sensitive—a tiny bird that could be ruined by 5 minutes too long in the oven . To make the best of a quail cover the breast with a little fat bacon and place the bird on a round of fried bread to cook. The bread soaks up the juices as the bird cooks, and is served as part of the finished dish.

To achieve best results with each type of bird, vary the oven temperature according to the chart. Baste where recommended, add extra fat to those birds that are exceptionally lean. Cover or partially cover with foil according to the recipe, for even cooking.

Preparing Poultry for Roasting
If the bird is frozen allow it to thaw completely before cooking (see page 149).

Wash the bird inside and out, and dry on absorbent kitchen paper. If it is to be stuffed, put the

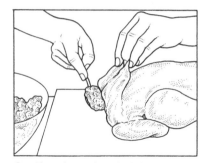

Stuffing the neck end of the bird

stuffing in the neck end only. If placed in the body cavity, stuffing can prevent the bird cooking through thoroughly, which is a health risk. Pull the skin lightly over the stuffing and truss the bird neatly to keep it a good shape. If you are not using stuffing, you can add extra flavour by putting half an onion or an apple inside the body cavity (this will not slow the cooking) and seasoning the inside well. Lean birds such as young chickens might benefit from a little butter flavoured with lemon rind or herbs inside the cavity.

Add any extra fat to the breast—softened butter or chicken fat are ideal, or rashers of streaky bacon—and cover if you wish. Or you can cover towards the end of

POULTRY ROASTING CHART

Chicken and Capon	190°C (375°F) mark 5	20 minutes per 450 g (1 lb) plus 20 minutes
Duck	190°C (375°F) mark 5	20 minutes per 450 g (1 lb)
Guinea fowl	190°C (375°F) mark 5	45–60 minutes
Goose	220°C (425°F) mark 7 Then reduce to 180°C (350°F) mark 4 and cover breast	20 minutes 13–15 minutes per 450 g (1 lb)
Quail	180°C (350°F) mark 4	20 minutes

TURKEY

Oven-ready weight (including stuffing if used)	Hours at 170°C (325°F) mark 3	Hours at 230°C (450°F) mark 8
2.7–3.6 kg (6–8 lb)	3–3½	2¼–2½
3.6–4.5 kg (8–10 lb)	3½–3¾	2½–2¾
4.5–5.4 kg (10–12 lb)	3¾–4	2¾
5.4–6.3 kg (12–14 lb)	4–4¼	3
6.3–7.3 kg (14–16 lb)	4¼–4½	3–3¼
7.3–8.2 kg (16–18 lb)	4½–4¾	3¼–3½
8.2–9 kg (18–20 lb)	4¾–5	3½–3¾
9–10 kg (20–22 lb)	5–5¼	3¾–4

the cooking time if the breast is browning too quickly. Preheat the oven and have the bird at room temperature before it goes in. Time the cooking according to the chart. For French-roasted birds add a little stock or wine to the roasting tin for basting.

To test when poultry is cooked: Insert a meat thermometer into the thickest part of the meat. When cooked the thermometer reading should be 88°C (190°F). Or, insert a skewer into the thickest part; on withdrawing it the juices should be clear.

ROAST CHICKEN

Serves 4

1.6–1.8 kg (3½–4 lb) chicken
herb stuffing (see page 155)
1 onion, skinned (optional)
1 thick lemon wedge (optional)
knob of butter (optional)
oil or melted butter
salt and freshly ground pepper
streaky bacon rashers, rinded

1 Wash the inside of the bird and stuff it at the neck end with the herb stuffing. To add flavour put an onion, lemon wedge or knob of butter in the body of the chicken.

2 Brush the bird with oil or melted butter, sprinkle it with salt and pepper and put it in a shallow roasting tin. Lay streaky bacon over the breast to prevent it becoming too dry.

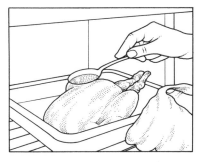

3 Cook in the oven at 190°C (375°F) mark 5, basting from time to time and allowing 20 minutes per 450 g (1 lb), plus 20 minutes. Put a piece of grease-proof paper over the breast if the skin becomes too brown. Alternatively, wrap the chicken in foil before roasting; allow the same cooking time but open the foil for the final 15–20 minutes to allow the chicken to brown.

4 Serve with bacon rolls, force-meat balls (see page 155), small sausages, bread sauce (see page 158) and thin gravy.

FRENCH ROAST CAPON

Serves 8

75 g (3 oz) butter
salt and freshly ground pepper
3.6 kg (8 lb) capon
5–6 sprigs tarragon or parsley
melted butter
2 bacon rashers, rinded
300 ml (½ pint) chicken stock

1 Cream the butter with salt and pepper and put inside capon with the herbs. Truss firmly.

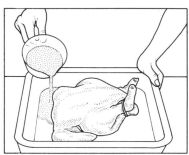

2 Brush the breast with melted butter and cover with bacon. Put in roasting tin, add the stock.

3 Roast at 190°C (375°F) mark 5 for 3 hours, basting often. Remove bacon for last 15 minutes.

ROAST QUAIL

Serves 4

4 rounds of fried bread
4 quail
2 bacon rashers, cut into strips

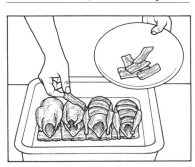

1 Put fried bread in a roasting tin. Place quail on bread and cover breasts with the bacon.

2 Roast in the oven at 180°C (350°F) mark 4 for about 20 minutes, basting with butter.

3 Serve on the bread with the bacon; thin gravy, fried crumbs and chipped potatoes are usual accompaniments.

ROAST DUCK

Serves 4

1.8 kg (4 lb) duck
sage and onion stuffing (see page 155)
salt and freshly ground pepper
15 ml (1 tbsp) flour
600 ml (1 pint) duck stock

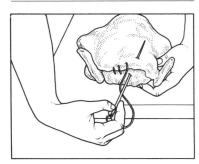

1 Wash the duck and dry it completely with absorbent kitchen paper. Spoon the stuffing into the neck end and truss the duck. Weigh it and calculate cooking time, allowing 20 minutes per 450 g (1 lb).

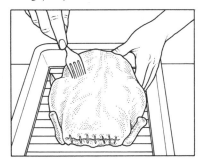

2 Put the duck on a wire rack in a roasting tin and sprinkle the breast liberally with a mixture of salt and pepper. Rub the seasoning thoroughly into the skin. Prick the skin all over with a sharp fork or skewer to allow fat to escape.

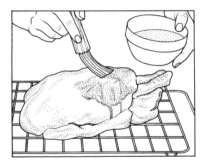

3 Roast at 190°C (375°F) mark 5 for the calculated cooking time, basting occasionally with the fat in the tin.

4 While the duck is cooking, strain the stock into a pan and bring to the boil. Boil rapidly until reduced to about 300 ml ($\frac{1}{2}$ pint). Cool and skim the fat off the surface of the liquid.

5 When the duck is cooked, a skewer pushed into the meat should release clear, not pink, juices. Transfer to a warm plate, remove the trussing string and keep hot.

6 Drain the fat from the roasting tin and stir the flour into the remaining juices. Cook over moderate heat until it bubbles, stirring all the time to prevent it sticking.

7 Gradually stir in the reduced stock. Cook the gravy for about 10 minutes, stirring until smooth and thickened. Season to taste and serve with the duck.

ROAST GOOSE

Serves 6

1 goose

salt

1 sour apple (optional)

1 apple, cored and cut into rings, lemon juice and oil, to garnish (optional)

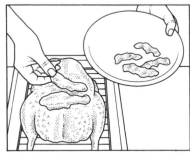

1 Wash and dry the goose. Prick the skin all over with a fork. Sprinkle the bird with salt and put it on a rack in a roasting tin. Cover the goose with the fat taken from inside. Place a sour apple in the roasting tin if you wish.

2 Roast the goose at 220°C (425°F) mark 7 for 20 minutes. Then reduce the temperature to 180°C (350°F) mark 4, cover the breast with greaseproof paper and roast for 13–15 minutes per 450 g (1 lb). Remove the paper during the last 30 minutes to allow the bird to brown.

3 Spoon off the fat from the tin and make giblet gravy (see page 157) with the remaining juices. Serve the goose with gravy and, if you wish, with apple rings that have been dipped in lemon juice, brushed with oil and lightly grilled. The goose may also be served with apple sauce (see page 158).

BOHEMIAN ROAST GOOSE

Serves 8–10

two 566-g (1$\frac{1}{4}$-lb) cans sauerkraut

4–5 kg (9–11 lb) goose

225 g (8 oz) apples, peeled, cored and cut into cubes

5 ml (1 tsp) salt

2.5 ml ($\frac{1}{2}$ tsp) caraway seeds

1 Put the sauerkraut with its liquid in a large saucepan and bring to the boil. Reduce the heat, cover and simmer for 30 minutes. Drain and rinse with cold water; drain again.

2 Wash and dry the goose. Prick the skin with a fork in several places. Add the apples, salt and caraway seeds to the sauerkraut and spoon into the neck end of the goose. Skewer the neck skin to the back of the goose and truss.

3 Put the goose breast side up on a rack in a roasting tin and roast in the oven at 220°C (425°F) mark 7 for 20 minutes, then reduce the temperature to 180°C (350°F) mark 4, cover the breast with greaseproof paper and roast for 4 hours or until tender. Remove the paper during the last 30 minutes to allow the bird to brown. Let the goose stand at room temperature for 15 minutes, so that it is easier to carve.

ROAST STUFFED TURKEY

Serves 8–10

4.5–5.5 kg (10–12 lb) turkey
chestnut stuffing (see page 155)
melted dripping or butter
salt and freshly ground pepper

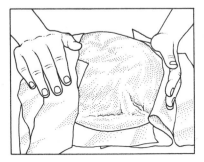

1 Remove the giblets and wash the bird. Drain well and dry with absorbent kitchen paper. Stuff the neck end of the turkey with chestnut stuffing taking care not to pack it too tightly. Cover the stuffing smoothly with the neck skin.

2 With the bird breast side up, fold the wing tips neatly under the body, catching in the neck skin. Truss the bird and tie the legs together. Make the body as plump and even in shape as possible. Weigh it and calculate the cooking time according to the chart on page 137.

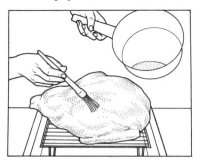

3 Put the bird breast side up on a rack in a roasting tin. Brush with the melted fat and season well with salt and pepper.

4 Cover the bird loosely with foil; roast at 230°C (450°F) mark 8 for the calculated cooking time until tender.

5 Remove the foil and baste 30 minutes before the end of cooking time. Serve with giblet gravy (see page 157) and cranberry sauce (see page 158).

BONED AND STUFFED ROAST TURKEY

Serves 16

4.5 kg (10 lb) turkey, boned (see page 153)
100 g (4 oz) butter or margarine, softened
salt and freshly ground pepper
watercress sprigs, to garnish
For the apricot and ginger stuffing
700-g (1½-lb) can apricot halves, drained, or 300 g (12 oz) dried apricots, soaked overnight
12 pieces of stem ginger
350 g (12 oz) fresh white breadcrumbs
175 g (6 oz) shredded suet
3 large eggs (size 2), beaten
salt and freshly ground pepper

1 Make the stuffing. Chop the apricots and ginger finely and mix with the breadcrumbs and suet. Bind with the egg and season to taste.

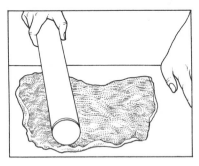

2 Lay the boned turkey skin side down on a board and pound to even thickness with a meat mallet or rolling pin.

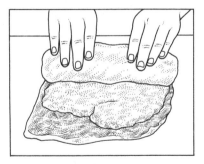

3 Cover the surface of the meat with the apricot and ginger stuffing and carefully roll it up. Do not roll too tightly or the stuffing will burst out during cooking.

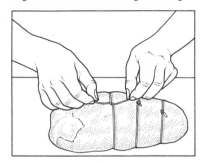

4 Tie the roll at intervals with fine string, or sew it up using a trussing needle. Weigh the stuffed roll and calculate the cooking time, allowing 35–40 minutes per 450 g (1 lb) prepared weight.

5 Put the roll skin side up in a roasting tin and spread with the softened fat. Cover with foil and roast in the oven at 170°C (325°F) mark 3 until 30 minutes before the end of the calculated cooking time.

6 Remove the foil and baste the turkey well with the juices in the tin. Increase the oven temperature to 220°C (425°F) mark 7. Pour off the excess fat and return the tin to the oven to roast for a further 30 minutes.

7 To serve, place the turkey roll on a serving dish and remove the strings. Garnish with watercress. Serve hot or cold.

ROAST DUCK WITH CRANBERRY GLAZE

Serves 4

two 1.6 kg (3½ lb) ducks

175 ml (6 fl oz) water

salt

flour for dredging

30 ml (2 tbsp) cornflour

30 ml (2 tbsp) lemon juice

60 ml (4 tbsp) red wine

396-g (14-oz) jar whole berry cranberry sauce

watercress sprigs, to garnish

1 Put the duck giblets and water in a saucepan. Cover, and simmer for 1 hour.

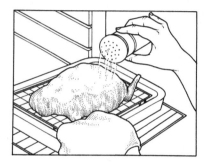

2 Wash and dry the ducks. Prick the skin and rub well with salt. Place on a rack in a roasting tin and roast at 190°C (375°F) mark 5 for 20 minutes per 450 g (1 lb), basting occasionally. About 15 minutes before the end of cooking time, baste, dredge with flour and finish at 220°C (425°F) mark 7.

3 Meanwhile, blend the cornflour, lemon juice and wine and stir in the strained giblet stock. Heat the cranberry sauce until softened, add the cornflour mixture and bring to the boil, stirring. Simmer for 3–4 minutes. Pour two thirds into a sauceboat and keep warm. Strain remaining sauce into a clean saucepan.

4 Spoon the fat from the roasting juices and add the juices to the strained sauce; boil rapidly until reduced to a rich glaze. Brush over the ducks in the tin.

5 Halve the ducks, arrange them on a serving dish and pour any remaining glaze over them. Garnish with watercress and serve with the cranberry sauce.

'BRICK' COOKERY

One of the favourite ways of cooking in the days of open fires was by encasing the meat in a coating of wet clay and baking the whole package in the embers. When baked the hard clay could be cracked off and the meat was revealed, moist, tender and full of flavour. The modern equivalent of this is cooking in a 'chicken brick'.

A chicken brick is made of unglazed clay and shaped more or less to the contours of a chicken. The porous clay absorbs steam from the chicken as it cooks, so that the effect is to roast it rather than to steam or boil. But because the food is covered, the juices are plentiful and the meat moist. There is no spitting and there is less evaporation than from an uncovered tin.

To prepare your brick the first time you use it, soak it in cold water for 30 minutes. After that a 10-minute soak is needed each time. This water soaked into the porous clay is what stops the chicken drying during cooking.

To prepare the chicken, rub the breast lightly with oil and a little salt. Put an onion or a lemon wedge in the body cavity for extra flavour if you wish. Then put the

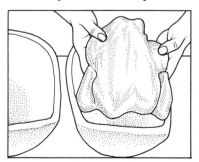

Putting chicken into soaked brick

chicken into the soaked brick and put the top on. Put the brick into a *cold* oven and set the temperature at 250°C (450°F) mark 8. Don't put the brick into a hot oven or it will crack; it must heat up gradually. Likewise, when you take it out of the oven put it on a board, not on metal or laminate.

Bake a 1.8 kg (4 lb) chicken for 1½ hours. Bake chicken portions

Pouring off the juices

for 1 hour. For extra crispness, pour off the juices and return the brick to the oven uncovered for 10 minutes at the end of the cooking time. Serve the chicken with gravy made from the juices.

Poultry casseroles can also be cooked in the brick, but the results are little different from cooking in a conventional casserole, and cleaning the brick after cooking with a sauce is rather difficult.

After cooking, don't leave the empty brick to cool and dry. When the chicken is removed, immerse the brick at once in *hot* water with no soap (clay may retain the soapy taste) and leave it to soak until convenient. Then scrub with a brush to remove stuck-on food and marks. The brick will never look really clean again, because of its unglazed surface, but if it is well scrubbed it is quite hygienic. If you find the smell or flavour of the cooked food lingers on, soak it in salt or vinegar solution for a few hours.

POACHING

Gentle simmering in plenty of water, with vegetables and herbs for flavour, is the perfect way to cook a chicken that is not tender enough to roast. 'Boiled chicken' is the term traditionally used, but the water must never boil, as this would toughen the connective tissues and dry out the meat.

For the best flavour in a poached dish, choose a 'boiling fowl'; this will be an older, tougher chicken than a roaster, with a more pronounced flavour. A roasting chicken can be poached, but reduce the cooking time.

Turkey can also be poached, though usually in joints because the size of the whole bird demands such a large pot. Duck and goose are not usually poached.

For tender, succulent meat, bring the water just to the boil, then reduce the heat and maintain it at no more than a gentle, bubbling simmer. After cooking, strain the stock and use it for a sauce to serve with the meat, or save it for soup. If you are cooking joints, include the backbone for extra flavour, straining it out afterwards.

BOILED CHICKEN WITH PARSLEY SAUCE

Serves 6

1.8 kg (4 lb) boiling fowl
$\frac{1}{2}$ lemon
salt
1 onion, skinned and stuck with 3–4 cloves
1 carrot, peeled
1 bouquet garni
For the sauce
20 g ($\frac{3}{4}$ oz) butter or margarine
30 ml (2 tbsp) flour
150 ml ($\frac{1}{4}$ pint) milk
15–30 ml (1–2 tbsp) chopped parsley
salt and freshly ground pepper

1 Clean the chicken and truss firmly. Rub skin with a lemon half to preserve the white colour.

2 Put the chicken into a large saucepan with some salt, the onion, carrot and bouquet garni and add water to cover. Bring to the boil, cover and simmer for about 3 hours for a boiling fowl, 1 hour for a younger bird.

3 Drain the chicken, remove the strings and keep it hot while making the sauce. Strain the cooking stock and reserve.

4 For the sauce, melt the fat in a small saucepan and blend in the flour. Cook over a gentle heat, stirring, until the mixture begins to bubble. Gradually stir in the milk and 150 ml ($\frac{1}{4}$ pint) of the chicken stock. Bring to the boil, stirring, and cook for 1–2 minutes until smooth and thickened. Add the parsley but do not re-boil or the sauce may turn green. Adjust the seasoning and serve with the boiled chicken.

CHICKEN FRICASSEE

Serves 4

1.1 kg (2$\frac{1}{2}$ lb) boiling fowl, jointed
2 onions, skinned and chopped
2 carrots, peeled and sliced
100 g (4 oz) mushrooms, sliced
1 bouquet garni
salt and freshly ground pepper
50 g (2 oz) butter or margarine
50 g (2 oz) flour
1 egg yolk
45 ml (3 tbsp) double cream
juice of $\frac{1}{2}$ a lemon
4 bacon rolls, grilled, and parsley sprigs, to garnish

1 Put the chicken and vegetables into a large saucepan with enough water to cover. Add the bouquet garni, salt and pepper. Bring to the boil, cover and simmer gently for 1$\frac{1}{2}$ hours, or until the chicken is tender.

2 Strain the stock; reserve the vegetables and stock separately. If you wish, remove the skin from the chicken. Carve the meat and cut it into cubes.

3 Melt the fat, stir in the flour and cook for 2–3 minutes. Remove from the heat and gradually add 600 ml (1 pint) stock. Bring to the boil and cook until the sauce thickens, stirring constantly. Add the meat and vegetables; remove from the heat.

4 Beat the egg yolk and cream together, add a little sauce and blend well. Return the mixture to the sauce and heat through without boiling. Add the lemon juice.

5 Pour into a serving dish and garnish with the grilled bacon rolls and parsley sprigs.

CASSEROLING

Casseroles of chicken and other poultry are amongst the tastiest dishes invented. Long slow cooking in a good stock or other flavoursome liquid will make any bird tender enough to cut with a fork. The addition of vegetables, herbs and other ingredients gives an extra dimension of flavour that can be varied endlessly.

Poultry can be casseroled whole, if small, or in portions. The meat from a very large bird such as a turkey is often removed from the bones and cut into cubes for more convenient cooking. The skin may be left on or removed, as you prefer. All types of poultry are good casseroled, though expensive quail and tender baby poussins are generally reserved for plainer methods. The joy of casseroling is that it can turn a bird of doubtful quality into a dish that will satisfy the most demanding gourmet.

To prepare poultry for casseroling, rinse and dry it as usual. Joint it if appropriate. In many recipes for casseroles the meat is first fried in a little oil, butter or margarine to seal in the juices and give a good golden colour. If you use reduced chicken or duck fat, it will give the dish even more flavour. Frying can be done either in the casserole, if it is flameproof, or in

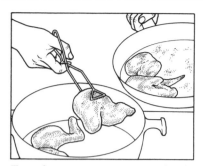

Transferring meat to ovenproof dish

a frying pan and the meat transferred to an ovenproof dish for cooking. The vegetables may also be browned or softened in the hot fat before adding to the meat.

Then, with all the ingredients in the pot, liquid is added; the amount varies from a few spoonfuls if the meat is likely to be tender and juicy itself, to much larger quantities for tougher meats that will require longer cooking. In addition to stock, wine or cider are popular cooking liquids, adding a luxurious flavour.

The oven temperature should be low so that the liquid in the pot never boils, but maintains a gentle simmer. If you have a heavy pot with a tightly fitting lid you can also cook a casserole very gently on top of the stove.

Once the poultry is tender the casserole may be ready to serve just as it is. With some dishes the sauce will need thickening, or the meat can be removed and the sauce boiled to reduce it and concentrate the flavour. If the bird is portioned or the meat cut in cubes, serve straight from the cooking pot. For a whole bird you will need to transfer it to a carving dish for serving, with the sauce in a separate bowl; or you may carve the bird in the kitchen, returning it to the original pot for serving.

CHICKEN IN A POT

Serves 6

| 25 g (1 oz) butter or margarine |
| 225 g (8 oz) carrots, peeled and sliced |
| 225 g (8 oz) small onions, skinned |
| 100 g (4 oz) streaky bacon, rinded and cut in small pieces |
| 1 lemon |
| large pinch of thyme |
| 1 garlic clove, skinned |
| 1.8 kg (4 lb) chicken |
| salt and freshly ground pepper |
| 450 g (1 lb) Jerusalem artichokes |
| chopped parsley, to garnish |

1 Using a flameproof casserole a little larger than the chicken, melt the fat and sauté the carrots, onions and bacon for 10 minutes until browned.

2 Pare the lemon and add the rind to the pan. Stir in the thyme and garlic. Remove the mixture from the pan.

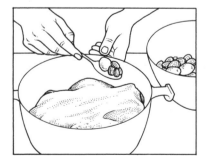

3 Put the chicken in the casserole, spoon the vegetables around it and season lightly. Cover and cook in the oven at 150°C (300°F) mark 2 for 2 hours.

4 Just before the 2 hours are up, peel the artichokes, putting them in salted water to prevent discoloration. When all the artichokes are peeled, drain them and add to the casserole, mixing them gently with the other vegetables.

5 Return the casserole to the oven without its lid, and cook for a further 30 minutes, until the chicken is tender.

6 Remove from the oven; transfer the chicken to a warmed serving dish and spoon the vegetables around it. Keep hot while you reduce the juices.

7 Discard the garlic and lemon rind from the casserole; skim the fat from the juices and boil the juices until reduced by half.

8 Spoon the reduced cooking juices over the chicken and vegetables on the serving dish and sprinkle chopped parsley generously over the top.

TURKEY IN CIDER

Serves 4–6

15 ml (1 tbsp) vegetable oil

1.1–1.4 kg (2½–3 lb) turkey legs

450 ml (¾ pint) chicken stock

1 large onion, skinned and thinly sliced

7.5 ml (1½ tsp) salt

1.25 ml (¼ tsp) freshly ground pepper

40 g (1½ oz) flour

150 ml (5 fl oz) single cream

25 g (1 oz) butter or margarine

175 g (6 oz) mushrooms, sliced

75 ml (5 tbsp) finely chopped parsley

300 ml (½ pint) dry cider

1 Heat the oil in a large saucepan and fry the turkey legs until well browned all over. Add the stock, onion, salt and pepper and bring to the boil. Reduce the heat, cover and simmer for 1½–2 hours, or until the meat is tender.

2 Remove the turkey legs from the pan and allow to cool slightly. Discard the skin, carve the meat off the bones and cut into 2.5-cm (1-inch) pieces. Meanwhile, boil the cooking stock rapidly until it is reduced to 175 ml (6 fl oz).

3 Blend the flour with half the cream and gradually add to the turkey stock, stirring all the time until smooth. Stir in the remaining cream and cook the sauce over a gentle heat until it boils and thickens, stirring well all the time.

4 Melt the fat in a small pan and sauté the sliced mushrooms until tender. Add them to the sauce with the turkey meat and 60 ml (4 tbsp) of the parsley. Stir in the cider and heat through.

5 Spoon the turkey mixture into a warmed serving dish and garnish with remaining parsley.

DUCK AND ORANGE CASSEROLE

Serves 4

1.8–2.6 kg (4–6 lb) duck, jointed

seasoned flour

knob of rendered duck fat or butter

100 g (4 oz) mushrooms, sliced

2 onions, skinned and chopped

25 g (1 oz) flour

450 ml (¾ pint) duck or chicken stock

150 ml (¼ pint) orange juice

1 orange

1 Coat the duck joints with seasoned flour. Heat the fat in a frying pan and fry the duck joints for 8–10 minutes, until brown, then transfer to a casserole.

2 Fry the mushrooms and onions lightly in the fat in the pan, then add to the casserole.

3 Stir the flour into the fat in the pan and brown it over low heat, stirring all the time. Off heat, stir in stock and juice.

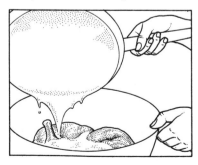

4 Return the pan to the heat and bring the sauce to the boil, stirring; continue to stir until it thickens then pour over the duck.

5 Cover the casserole and cook in the oven at 180°C (350°F) mark 4 for 1 hour, or until the duck is tender.

6 Pare off the coloured part of the orange rind with a vegetable peeler and cut it into very thin strips. Divide the orange itself into segments, removing any pith or pips.

7 Simmer the strips of rind in water until tender—about 5 minutes; drain well and sprinkle over the cooked duck joints. Garnish with the orange segments.

CHICKEN WITH MINT

Serves 4

25 g (1 oz) butter

4 chicken quarters, halved and skinned, 900 g (2 lb) total weight

900 g (2 lb) potatoes, peeled and thinly sliced

225 g (8 oz) leeks, roughly chopped

30 ml (2 tbsp) chopped fresh mint or 10 ml (2 tsp) dried

15 ml (1 tbsp) flour

salt and freshly ground pepper

60 ml (4 tbsp) chicken stock

chopped fresh mint or parsley, to garnish

1 Heat the butter in a large frying pan, add the chicken quarters, two at a time, and fry until well browned.

2 In a deep, buttered 1.7-litre (3-pint) casserole, layer the potato, chicken and leeks with the mint and flour. Season well between each layer. Finish with a layer of potato. Pour over the chicken stock.

3 Cover the casserole tightly and bake in the oven at 170°C (325°F) mark 3 for 1 hour. Uncover and cook for about a further 30 minutes until the chicken is tender and the top brown. Serve garnished with chopped fresh mint or parsley.

CROCKPOT COOKING

Cooking in a crockpot or electric casserole is a modern extension of the principle of casseroling. By cooking at a low, even temperature for long periods, the foods become tender and flavours blend to give tasty meals with the minimum of trouble and attention.

When cooking poultry in an electric casserole, cut it into small joints and remove all the skin. Be sure frozen poultry is completely thawed before cooking starts.

Some manufacturers state that pre-frying the meat and vegetables is not necessary, but results are much better if you do take the trouble to do this. Fry the poultry pieces and vegetables in a separate pan for 5–10 minutes before putting them in the slow cooker, to give them a good golden colour and seal in the juices and flavour. Stir the stock or cooking liquid into the frying pan, scraping any sediment from the base, and bring that to the boil before you pour it over the poultry.

Once you have done this, you should generally not lift the lid of the casserole until cooking is complete. If you need to add extra ingredients towards the end of the time, allow for the heat loss and increase the cooking time; keep the lid off the casserole for as short a time as possible by adding the fresh ingredients quickly. Don't add frozen vegetables to the slow cooker as they bring down the

temperature too much.

Test if the poultry is cooked by piercing with a sharp knife. If more cooking is required replace the lid and cook for at least another hour.

Thickening: To thicken the sauce, either toss the poultry pieces in seasoned flour before pre-frying or blend a little corn-flour or flour to a smooth paste with cold water and stir it into the electric casserole at the end of the cooking process. If the dish has been cooked on a high setting the sauce will thicken immediately; on low setting you will need to replace the lid and cook for a further 10–15 minutes.

Adapting recipes

You can cook all your favourite poultry casserole recipes in the electric casserole, but remember to remove all skin and use only about two thirds of the normal quantity of liquid unless rice, pasta or dried beans are to be added at the end.

CREAMED CHICKEN WITH GINGER AND CELERY

Serves 4

40 g (1½ oz) flour
15 ml (1 tbsp) paprika
salt and freshly ground pepper
2.5 ml (½ tsp) ground ginger
4 chicken portions, skinned
50 g (2 oz) butter
15 ml (1 tbsp) vegetable oil
1 medium onion, skinned and chopped
4 sticks of celery, trimmed
225 g (8 oz) button mushrooms
225 g (8 oz) tomatoes, skinned and chopped
450 ml (¾ pint) chicken stock
150 ml (¼ pint) white wine
175 g (6 oz) spaghetti, broken up
142 ml (5 fl oz) soured cream
chopped chives, to garnish

1 Stir the flour, paprika, seasoning and ginger together and coat the chicken portions with the mixture.

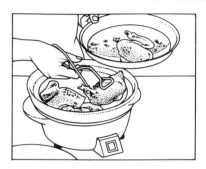

2 Heat the butter and oil in a large frying pan and fry the chicken for 10 minutes until golden brown all over. Remove and place in the casserole.

3 Fry the onion, celery, mushrooms and tomatoes for 2–3 minutes, add the stock and wine and bring to the boil. Pour into the electric casserole.

4 Place the lid in position and cook on high for 3–4 hours or low for 6–8 hours.

5 About 45 minutes before the end of cooking time, turn the electric casserole to high, add the pieces of spaghetti, replace lid and cook until chicken is tender. Stir in cream, garnish and serve.

PRESSURE COOKING

Small birds and poultry joints can be cooked very quickly in a pressure cooker. Use any casserole or poaching recipe.

When cooking a casserole, brown the bird or pieces in hot fat in the pressure cooker, without the trivet. Remove and brown or soften any vegetables. Return the poultry to the cooker, using the vegetables as a bed to keep the bird off the base of the cooker. Add the liquid, according to the weight and cooking time (see chart).

Then put on the lid and bring the cooker to high (15 lb) pressure. Cook for the required time and reduce pressure quickly by placing cooker in a bowl of cold water and running cold water over it.

If the sauce needs thickening, use a little flour mixed with an equal quantity of softened butter. Place the open cooker over the heat and whisk the paste a little at a time into the sauce.

For poaching, stand poultry on the trivet and add vegetables and water. Cook according to the chart. Reduce pressure as above and strain the stock for use in a sauce if wished.

Adding liquid: Calculate the cooking time by the chart. Allow 300 ml ($\frac{1}{2}$ pint) liquid for up to 900 g (2 lb) poultry for the first 15 minutes cooking, then add 150 ml ($\frac{1}{4}$ pint) for every 450 g (1 lb) weight.

GUIDE TO COOKING TIMES IN A PRESSURE COOKER

Chicken	spring and poussin	4–6 minutes per 450 g (1 lb)
	roasting 1.1–1.3 kg ($2\frac{1}{2}$–$3\frac{1}{2}$ lb)	6–8 minutes per 450 g (1 lb)
	boiling fowl 2.2 kg (5 lb)	10–12 minutes per 450 g (1 lb)
	3.1 kg (7 lb) halved	10–12 minutes per 450 g (1 lb)
	joints or pieces	4–6 minutes
Turkey	joints or pieces	10–15 minutes
Duck	whole 1.3 kg ($3\frac{1}{2}$ lb)	6–8 minutes per 450 g (1 lb)
	halved 2–2.7 kg ($4\frac{1}{4}$–6 lb)	4–5 minutes per 450 g (1 lb)
Guinea fowl	whole 700 g ($1\frac{1}{2}$ lb)	6–8 minutes per 450 g (1 lb)
	halved or jointed	4–5 minutes per 450 g (1 lb)

CHICKEN WITH TARRAGON SAUCE

Serves 4

5 ml (1 tsp) salt

freshly ground pepper

25 g (1 oz) butter

a few fresh tarragon leaves, chopped (stalks reserved)

1.4 kg (3 lb) chicken, with giblets

15 ml (1 tbsp) lemon juice

1 medium onion, skinned

1 bay leaf

600 ml (1 pint) water

3 egg yolks

150 ml (5 fl oz) double cream

30 ml (2 tbsp) dry white wine

lemon wedges and extra tarragon leaves, to garnish

2 Put the trivet in the pressure cooker and stand the chicken and giblets on it. Add the onion, bay leaf and tarragon stalks. Pour on the water and put on the lid.

3 Bring to high (15 lb) pressure. Cook for about 20 minutes.

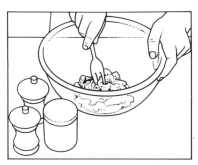

1 Mash the salt and pepper with the butter and tarragon. Rub chicken with the lemon juice and put butter mixture in body cavity.

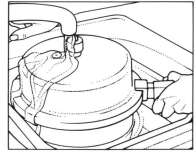

4 Place the cooker in a bowl of cold water and run cold water over it to reduce pressure. Lift out the bird on to a plate.

5 Strain the stock, measure 450 ml (¾ pint) into a saucepan and heat. Whisk together the egg yolks, cream and wine. Remove the stock from the heat, stir in the egg and cream mixture and continue to heat gently, stirring constantly until it thickens. Do not allow to boil. Adjust seasoning.

6 Pour the sauce over the whole chicken and leave to get cold. Carve the chicken and serve on a flat dish garnished with lemon wedges and tarragon leaves.

SPRING CHICKEN CASSEROLE

Serves 4

1.1 kg (2½ lb) chicken
25 g (1 oz) butter or margarine
2 medium onions, skinned and sliced
350 g (12 oz) small carrots, pared
396-g (14-oz) can of tomatoes
600 ml (1 pint) chicken stock
salt and freshly ground pepper
30 ml (2 tbsp) flour
For the parsley dumplings
100 g (4 oz) self raising flour
50 g (2 oz) shredded suet
1.25 ml (¼ tsp) salt
pinch of freshly ground pepper
15 ml (1 tbsp) chopped parsley
about 75 ml (5 tbsp) cold water

1 Cut the chicken into eight pieces and remove the skin. Melt the fat in the uncovered pressure cooker and fry the chicken pieces for 5–10 minutes until they are well browned. Remove the chicken and fry the onions until they are just golden.

2 Return the chicken to the cooker with the carrots, drained tomatoes (reserving the juice), stock and seasoning. Put on the lid and bring to high (15 lb) pressure. Cook for 4–6 minutes.

3 Mix the dumpling ingredients to a soft dough with the water. Divide into eight balls.

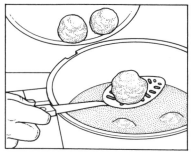

4 Reduce pressure quickly. Bring to boiling point, uncovered, and add the dumplings. Put on the lid and lower the heat to allow the cooker to steam gently for 3 minutes. Increase the heat to bring to low (5 lb) pressure and cook a further 4 minutes. Reduce pressure quickly.

5 Put chicken, vegetables and dumplings in a casserole. Blend the flour to a smooth cream with some of the tomato juice and stir in some of the cooking liquid. Add to the cooker and bring to the boil uncovered, stirring until thick. Pour over the chicken.

BRAISED TURKEY LEGS

Serves 4

4 streaky bacon rashers, rinded
4 turkey drumsticks
30 ml (2 tbsp) vegetable oil
2 medium onions, skinned and quartered
2 carrots, peeled and sliced
2 sticks of celery, trimmed and chopped
100 g (4 oz) mushrooms, sliced
450 ml (¾ pint) chicken or turkey stock
salt and freshly ground pepper
1 bouquet garni
15 ml (1 tbsp) tomato purée
30 ml (2 tbsp) cornflour

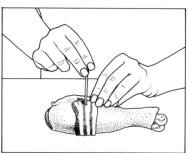

1 Wrap the bacon round the turkey and secure with cocktail sticks. Heat the oil in the uncovered cooker and fry until brown.

2 Remove, and brown the vegetables. Drain off the excess fat, stir in the stock, seasoning, bouquet garni and tomato purée. Put the turkey legs on the vegetables. Cover with the lid and bring to high (15 lb) pressure. Cook for 15 minutes.

3 Reduce pressure quickly. Discard bouquet garni and sticks. Put turkey and vegetables in a serving dish. Mix cornflour to a smooth cream with a little water and add a little cooking liquid.

4 Add the mixture to the cooker and bring to the boil uncovered, stirring until the gravy thickens. Pour over the turkey.

Choosing Poultry

With the different types of bird available — ranging from economical frozen chicken to luxurious fresh goose — and the many different ways they are sold, poultry is a popular choice for every sort of occasion. Use the information in this chapter to help you make exactly the right selection for the meals you cook.

BUYING POULTRY

By far the tastiest poultry to buy is that which has been farmyard reared and is freshly killed. But as with most things, the best is also the most expensive. For a more economical product, factory-reared chilled and frozen birds are generally of an acceptable quality.

Chicken and turkey are the most popular poultry and are readily available all year round. When buying a fresh chicken or turkey look for a plump, well-rounded breast, and skin that is free from blemishes and bruising.

When buying by weight, particularly a chicken, remember to check whether the giblets are with the bird; these weigh approximately 175 g (6 oz), which is a significant proportion of a bird weighing, say, 1.4 kg (3 lb) and will affect the number of portions you get after cooking. Don't reject the giblets, though, if available, as they make superb stock for gravy.

Other points to look for when buying frozen chicken and turkeys are whether the bird is already stuffed, 'butter-basted' or otherwise different from a straightforward dressed bird. All these pre-treated birds have their uses, but make sure they are what you want at that particular moment — if you need a bird for casseroling, you will not want it pre-stuffed.

The smallest chickens available are *poussins*, which are baby chickens weighing 350–450 g (12 oz–1 lb). One serves 1–2 people. Double poussins weigh 550–900 g ($1\frac{1}{4}$–2 lb) and will serve 3–4 people.

Most of the birds available are *broilers* weighing 1.1–1.6 kg ($2\frac{1}{2}$–$3\frac{1}{2}$ lb); these are suitable for all methods of cooking and serve 3–4 people. A *spring chicken* is a small broiler weighing 900 g–1.1 kg (2–$2\frac{1}{2}$ lb); one serves 2–3 people. Larger *roasting chickens* and *capons* (young cockerels that have been castrated and specially fattened) are available up to about 4.6 kg (10 lb), and will serve 6–10 people. *Boiling fowl*, not usually sold in supermarkets but available from traditional butchers and poulterers, are older, tougher birds weighing 1.8–3.2 kg (4–7 lb), and are excellent if poached or slowly casseroled.

Turkeys range in weight from about 2.6–14 kg (6–30 lb). A 4 kg (9 lb) oven-ready turkey is equivalent to one of about 5.4 kg (12 lb) undressed weight. Allow 275–350 g (10–12 oz) dressed weight per portion when estimating what size to buy.

When a whole bird is too large for your requirements, buy *chicken and turkey portions*. These range from boned and rolled joints ready for roasting and easy slicing, through halved and quartered birds, down to individual serving portions. You can also buy chicken livers, turkey sausages, burgers and packs of meat for casseroles, soups and stews.

Duck is widely available frozen or chilled and occasionally in portions. It is more difficult to buy a fresh farmyard duck than a chicken, as the demand is much less, but the flavour will be good if you can find one. Don't buy ducks weighing less than 1.4 kg (3 lb) as the proportion of bone to meat is excessively high in a small bird. Allow about 450 g (1 lb) dressed weight per portion. Again, look for a well-rounded, unblemished breast, but don't buy a duck that has noticeably large amounts of fat as the meat is very rich anyway.

Goose is largely a seasonal bird, though frozen geese can be bought throughout the year. It is advisable to order a goose in advance as butchers, poulterers and supermarkets tend not to keep large stocks. Birds range in size from about 3 kg (7 lb) to as much as 6.75 kg (15 lb). Allow 350–400 g (12–14 oz) dressed weight per portion.

Guinea fowl are available all the year round, and are obtainable both fresh and frozen. An average guinea fowl will serve 4 people. When buying, look out for a plump breast and smooth-skinned feet.

Quail are sold plucked but not drawn, as they are eaten whole. Allow one per person.

STORING POULTRY
To store fresh poultry remove the giblets from inside the bird (except quail) as soon as you get it home. Remove any tight packaging, cover the bird loosely with a bag, and store in the refrigerator for a maximum of 3 days. The giblets should preferably be cooked straight away as they deteriorate more quickly than the rest of the bird. If storing, keep separate from the rest of the bird.

Frozen poultry
Frozen chicken will keep in good condition in the freezer for up to a year, but the giblets will start to deteriorate after about 2 months. Commercially frozen chickens packed with the giblets in the cavity should therefore be cooked within 1–2 months of purchase. Frozen stuffed poultry should also be stored for up to 2 months.

Turkey with the giblets removed stores well for about 6 months, duck or goose (which are much fattier) store for 4–5 months.

To freeze fresh poultry, remove the giblets and pack them separately. Wrap the bird in heavy-duty

Padding poultry legs with foil

polythene, padding the legs with foil first so that they can't spike their way through the bag. Exclude as much air as possible before sealing and labelling.

To save space and provide you with individual portions when it comes to cooking, you may prefer to cut the bird into portions before

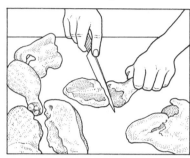
Cutting the bird into portions

freezing. Cut a chicken or turkey into quarters or into eight portions, halve ducks or guinea fowl. Wrap each joint individually in foil or polythene bags and then combine them in a larger package.

Freeze at the lowest temperature available in your freezer (ideally −32°C/−26°F); higher temperatures can give disappointing results. Remember to turn the temperature control down 24 hours before you intend to freeze the bird to give the cabinet time to get really cold. Once the bird is frozen return the control to the normal storage temperature.

Thawing poultry
Frozen poultry must be thawed completely before cooking. Poultry cooked from frozen, or even with a few ice crystals remaining, is a serious health risk.

Birds up to 2.7 kg (6 lb) should be thawed in the refrigerator. Larger birds should be thawed at room temperature (16–17°C/ 65–70°F). Do not thaw in the refrigerator as the process is too slow. Thaw the bird in its wrappings but open the bag and take any giblets from the cavity as soon as they can be moved. Once thawed, cook as soon as possible.

Approximate thawing times in the refrigerator
1.4 kg (3 lb) oven-ready   9 hours
2.3 kg (5 lb) oven-ready   15 hours
At room temperature
4.5 kg (10 lb) oven-ready   9 hours
6.8 kg (15 lb) oven-ready 24 hours
9 kg (20 lb) oven-ready   30 hours

Joints: Allow 6 hours.

Thawing in a microwave oven
Leave polythene wrappings in place but remove foil or wire ties.

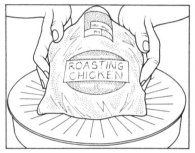
Placing bird in microwave-safe dish

Place whole package in a microwave-safe dish. Open end and remove the giblets as soon as they can be moved.
Whole chickens, ducks, geese, guinea fowl: 6–8 minutes per 450 g (1 lb) on low setting. Then close the wrappings and place the bird in cold water for 30 minutes.
Whole turkeys: 10–12 minutes per 450 g (1 lb) on low setting.
Joints: 4–7 minutes per 450 g (1 lb) on low setting. Then remove wrappings and place in cold water for 15 minutes.

Storing cooked poultry
Leftover roast poultry should be cooled as quickly as possible. Remove stuffing and wrap meat in polythene or foil before storing in the refrigerator. Eat within 3 days. Use cooked dishes within 1 day.

To freeze cooked poultry, cool quickly and remove any stuffing. Large joints are best removed from the bone. Pack portions in foil and overwrap with heavy-duty polythene. Store for 2 months.

Poultry Techniques

The way a bird is presented can transform the appearance of the finished dish. By mastering the basic skills which can be employed in preparing and serving poultry, you will be able to cope with a variety of exciting dishes and your guests will always be impressed. It's easy when you know how!

PREPARING POULTRY

To get the best out of poultry prepare it carefully before cooking. If any quills have been left behind after plucking (this is most likely with the large birds such as goose and turkey) remove them carefully with tweezers. If there are hairs left on the skin, singe them off with a lighted taper. Rinse all birds well, inside and out, in cold water and dry thoroughly with kitchen paper.

TRUSSING

Trussing keeps poultry in a good shape for roasting, making it more attractive on the table and easier to carve. Always remove the butcher's or packager's trussing so that you can wash and dry the bird, then truss it again yourself. A *trussing needle* (a long needle with a large eye) is useful, but failing this, use a skewer and fine string to truss the bird.

First fold the neck skin under the body and fold the tips of the wings back towards the backbone so that they hold the skin in position; set the bird on its back and press the legs well into the sides, raising and plumping the breast. Make a slit in the skin above the vent and put the tail (the 'parson's nose') through this.

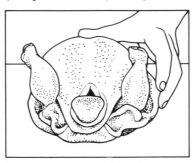

'Parson's nose' seen through slit

Thread the needle with fine string and insert it close to the second joint of the right wing; push it right through the body, passing it out so as to catch the

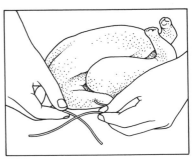

Tying the ends of string

corresponding joint on the left side. Insert the needle again in the first joint of the left wing, pass it through the flesh at the back of the body, catching the tips of the wings and the neck skin, and pass it out through the first joint of the wing on the right side. Tie the ends of the string in a bow.

To truss the legs, re-thread the needle and insert it through the gristle at the right side of the parson's nose. Pass the string over the right leg, under the back and over the left leg, through the gristle at the left side of the

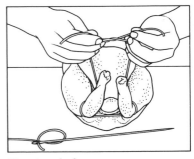

Trussing the legs

parson's nose. Carry it behind the parson's nose and tie the ends firmly together.

If using a skewer, insert it right through the body of the bird just below the thigh bone and turn the bird over on its breast. First,

Using a skewer to truss

catching in the wing tips, pass the string under the ends of the skewer and cross it over the back. Turn the bird over and tie the ends of the string together round the tail, securing the drumsticks.

JOINTING

Although poultry portions are readily available, jointing a bird yourself is cheaper and leaves you with bones and giblets for stock. Joint a chicken several hours before starting to cook a casserole so that you can make stock first. Or, if you have to use water for cooking, add the backbone to it.

Use a sharp, heavy knife or *poultry shears*. Start by trimming off the excess skin at the neck end and removing any chunks of fat from inside the body cavity. Cut off the knuckle ends from the legs, and the wing tips; use for stock.

With the bird breast side up, neck towards you, cut straight along one side of the breast bone from the vent to the neck. Spread open and cut along one side of the backbone to divide it in half. If your knife is not sharp enough, lay

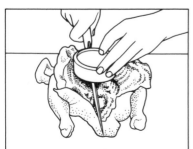

Breaking the bones with a weight

it along the cutting line and give the back of the knife a firm bang with a heavy weight to break the bones first. Then cut along the other side of the backbone and remove to use in the stock.

To quarter a chicken or guinea fowl cut each half in half again crossways between the breast and

Quartering poultry

the leg. To quarter a duck, leave plenty of breast meat with the leg portion as there is very little meat on the leg. For duck recipes using breast only, use all the breast and save the thin legs for pâté.

Large birds may require dividing again. The leg can be divided in two through the centre of the joint to give a thigh and a drumstick portion. The wing quarter can be divided to give a wing and a breast portion.

Alternative method

If you prefer to take the meat off the carcass rather than cutting right through the bones you will need a small sharp knife, sometimes known as a *filleting knife*.

Start with the chicken breast side up with the neck end towards you. Gently pull the leg away from the body and cut through the skin between the thigh and the breast; repeat on the other side of the bird. Turn the bird over and continue cutting through the skin around the legs, following the natural line of the thighs down towards the backbone. You will find a tiny succulent portion of meat where the backbone joins the thigh — the oyster. Loosen the oysters but don't detach yet. With

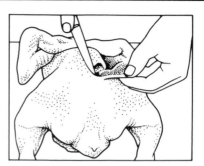

Loosening the oyster

bird on its back, push the legs outwards until the joints release. Turn the bird over, slip knife into joint and ease the legs away from the backbone, making sure oyster is still attached. Set aside.

Turn bird over, wings towards you. Cut through the skin and

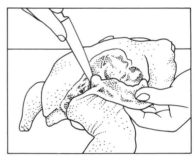

Working breast meat from bones

flesh along one side of the breast bone. With knife flat against rib cage, work breast from the bones, keeping the meat in one piece.

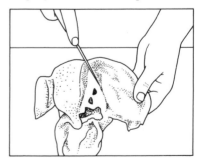

Bending wing away from carcass

Then grasp the wing firmly and bend it away from the carcass until

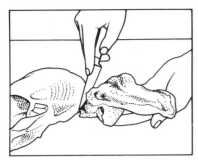

Cutting through sinews and tendons

the joint releases. Cut through any sinews and tendons and set the joint aside. Repeat on the other side. You are now left with a bare carcass that can be used for stock.

To make a *chicken 'suprême'* take the breast portion only, with no wing attached and remove the skin. With a sharp knife, cut and scrape the meat from the bones, gently pulling back the meat in one piece as you cut. Underneath the main breast meat is a thin fillet of meat only loosely attached to the rest; try not to separate this. Discard bones and cut out the white tendon that remains.

SPATCHCOCKING

Spatchcocking is a way of pre-paring a small whole bird for grill-ing. The bones are left in but the body is opened flat. Use for poussins, spring chickens and guinea fowl. You will need poultry shears or a sharp, heavy knife.

The easiest method is to lay the bird on its breast and cut along the centre of the backbone with shears. With a knife, work from inside

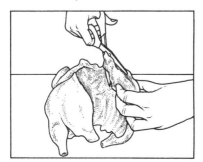

Cutting along the backbone

the cavity; insert the knife through the vent, put as much weight on it as you can and press down to break your way through the bone. The skin should remain attached to the bone on either side.

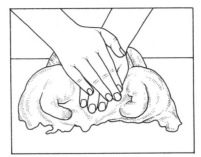

Flattening the bird with the hands

Force the two halves of the bird open with your hands, turn it over and lay it as flat as you can on a board. Then, with the heel of your hand, bang the centre of the bird firmly to break the breast bone, collar bones and wishbone. With a slightly bigger bird you may find this easier with the flat of a meat mallet or a rolling pin.

Although the body now seems quite flat, it will start to curl back into its natural shape as soon as the heat gets to it. To prevent this happening thread skewers across the body to hold it flat during cooking. Use two long skewers, one from leg to leg, the other from wing to wing and remove them before serving.

SKINNING

One of the joys of roast poultry is the crisp brown skin. But for recipes in which the skin is not crisped it is often nicer to remove the skin before cooking. Slimmers particularly will want to remove the skin as this is where most of the fat lies.

For a breast portion with no wing attached this is a simple matter, the skin will peel away easily. But wing and leg portions are not so easy as the skin is very firmly attached at the thin ends of the joints.

To help you keep a grip on the meat use a clean damp cloth and grasp the joint firmly. For a leg portion, first slip your fingers under the skin at the thigh end and loosen it all round. Grasp the

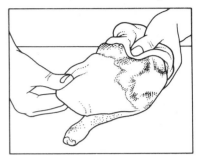

Peeling the skin off the joint

meaty part firmly with a cloth in one hand and peel the skin off the joint so that it is inside out. When you reach the point where it is bonded to the bone take a small sharp knife and slip it between skin and bone to cut the skin away cleanly.

On a wing portion, lift the skin away from the breast where it is loose and gently peel it away along the first wing bone as far as it will go. Then hold the meaty part firmly with a cloth in one hand, take your small sharp knife and, working with the tip, ease the skin away from the joint. There is very little meat on the second wing bone so the skin clings tightly. Slit the skin on the inside of the wing and gently peel it away all round. Cut off the wing tip just above the joint, taking all the skin with it.

BONING

With the bones removed, a chicken or duck makes a lovely meaty casing for stuffing and the resulting joint is easy to carve. A classic galantine or ballotine is made this way. The stuffed bird is shaped into a neat roll, stitched up securely with fine string and either roasted or poached. After cooking it is chilled and usually finished with a glaze of aspic or a creamy chaudfroid sauce.

Sometimes a ballotine is served hot with a rich accompanying sauce—very impressive for a party dish and much easier to carve in front of guests than a whole bird. Usually the stuffing is rich so that one bird will serve up to twice as many prepared this way rather than simply roasted.

Even more dramatic is the traditional quail inside a chicken, inside a goose—rarely served these days but a delight to imagine.

Another approach is to bone only the breast, leaving the leg and wing bones intact. This way the cavity can be generously filled with stuffing and the breast re-formed to its natural shape. This gives a finished dish that looks like the conventional roast poultry, but with an amount of stuffing that makes it go much further. The savoury flavours of the stuffing will permeate right through the breast flesh as it cooks.

Individual portions with the bones removed also make attractive casings for savoury fillings. *Chicken Kiev* is the example most people know—a boneless chicken breast with the wing bone attached; the breast meat is wrapped round a portion of garlic butter, and the whole thing is dipped in egg and bread-crumbs and deep-fried.

A leg portion with the bone removed can be filled in the same way; the end of the knuckle bone is usually left in place to give the joint shape and keep the end firmly closed.

Boning a whole bird

The secret of success is a sharp knife; a boning knife with a blade about 12.5–15 cm (5–6 inches) long would be a good one to choose. The procedure is the same for all birds even though the carcass shapes differ somewhat.

Lay the bird on a board breast side up. Cut off the wings at the second joint and the legs at the first. Turn the bird breast down.

Cut cleanly through the skin and flesh down the centre of the

back from vent to neck. Keeping the knife close to the carcass and slightly flattened to avoid damaging the flesh, carefully work

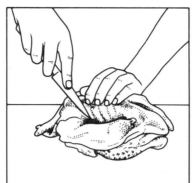

Exposing the wing joint

the flesh off the rib cage on one side of the bird until the wing joint is exposed; repeat on the other side to expose the other wing joint.

Take hold of the severed end of one wing joint. Scrape the knife over the bone backwards and forwards, working the flesh from the bone; try not to damage the

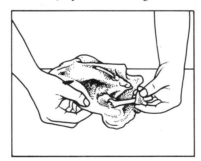

Drawing out the bone

skin. When the wing and socket are exposed, sever the ligaments with the point of the knife and draw out the bone. Repeat with the second wing.

Continue working the flesh off the main frame until the leg joint is exposed. Sever the ligaments attaching the bone to the body

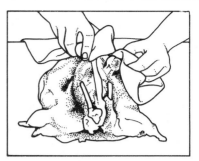

Breaking the leg joint

flesh and break the leg joint by twisting it firmly (use a cloth to get a good grip). Working from the body end of the leg, hold the end of the bone firmly and scrape away all the flesh from the thigh. Cut carefully round the joint with the point of the knife and scrape the drumstick clean in the same way. Pull the bone free. Repeat with the other leg.

Now go on to work the flesh from the rest of the main frame. Take care not to cut the skin over the breast bone, where the flesh becomes very thin, as the two halves of the breast must remain attached to each other.

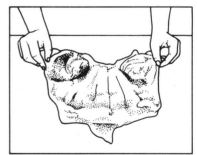

Laying the whole bird out flat

You can now lay the whole bird out flat ready to spread the stuffing over the cut surface.

Leaving the limbs on

If you want to leave the bones in the wings and legs, sever the appropriate joints with a knife as you reach them and continue round the carcass as before.

Boning a leg
With the point of a sharp knife cut round the end of the bone at the thigh end of the leg to free the

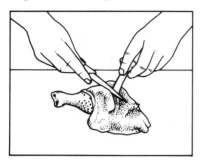

Scraping the flesh off the bone

flesh. Then grasp the end firmly and scrape the flesh carefully off the bone, taking care that you do not cut through the flesh. When you reach the joint use the point again to sever the ligaments all round. Scrape and work your way down the drumstick until you reach the knuckle. Cut off the bone joint above the knuckle and remove it.

CARVING
For perfect carving you need a long, sharp knife and a long-handled fork with two long prongs and a finger-guard. Place the bird on a flat carving dish or board—sides higher than about 1 cm ($\frac{1}{2}$ inch) will get in your way. Some carving dishes have spikes to hold the meat in place, some have a channel round the edge to drain the juices away from the standing bird or joint.

If you garnish the bird with vegetables or other trimmings to take it to the table, remove these before you start to carve so that you have room to work. If you have a large carving dish you can arrange the carved meat along the edge of the dish ready for serving; if using a smaller dish have another hot dish ready to take the slices as they are prepared. Carving on to individual plates is not ideal as you will not be able to mix dark and light meats in each serving.

Carving chicken and turkey
Place the bird on the dish so that one wing is towards your left hand with the breast diagonally towards

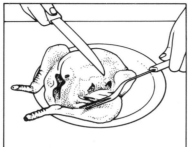

Prising the leg outwards with fork

you. Steadying the bird with the flat of the knife, prise the leg outwards with the fork, exposing the thigh joint. Cut through the joint to sever the leg. On a turkey or large chicken hold the end of the drumstick in one hand and cut slices from the leg in a downward slant away from you, turning the leg to get slices from all round the joint. When the bone is bare set it to one end of the dish. For a medium-sized chicken the leg will not have enough meat for carving but can be divided into two at the joint, giving a thigh and a drum-stick portion. If the chicken is small the leg may be served as a single portion.

Next remove the wing that is facing you. Hold the wing with the fork and cut through the outer layer of the breast into the joint. Ease the wing from the body and cut through the gristle. A turkey wing may be divided again; a chicken wing is too small and is served in one piece.

Carve the breast in thin slices parallel with the breast bone. If the bird is stuffed, the outer slices of meat and stuffing will carve together; the rest of the stuffing will have to be scooped out with a spoon. Carve one side of the carcass clean before turning the dish round and starting the pro-cess again on the other side of the bird.

Carving duck and goose
Duck and goose have particularly tough leg and wing ligaments and a shorter, heavier knife is needed to cut through these. Place bird on carving dish with legs diagonally

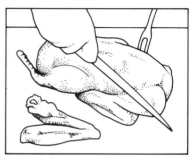

Cutting through wing joint

towards you. Hold the body firmly with the fork and cut down through the wing joint. Move fork closer to leg end and cut firmly through the joint. Leave a duck leg whole; separate a goose leg into two. With a long carving knife carve thin breast slices.

Jointing small cooked chickens and guinea fowl
Halve or quarter small chickens such as poussins, or guinea fowl. Use a strong, heavy knife and cut the bird in two straight through the breast and backbone. Halve each piece crossways for quarters.

Jointing a duckling
Place the bird on a board with the legs facing you. With poultry shears, cut along the top, keeping the blades just to one side of the breast bone. When you reach the wishbone, cut firmly through it and open up the bird. Next cut through the back, just to one side of the backbone. Cut down the other side and discard it.

Lay the two duckling halves skin side up on the board and with a sharp knife cut through the skin and flesh between the wing and leg sections. Leave plenty of breast meat with the leg portion. Use the shears to cut through the bone to divide the portions.

ACCOMPANIMENTS TO POULTRY

STUFFINGS

Stuffing, or forcemeat as it is sometimes known, serves a triple purpose. It fills the neck cavity of the bird, helping to keep the breast looking plump and well-rounded; it adds flavour to the meat and it extends the meat to give more servings.

Assemble the ingredients for a stuffing well ahead if you wish but don't mix in the liquid or egg as it tends to make the stuffing stodgy.

Don't put a meat stuffing in the bird until you are ready to cook. It is not safe to leave uncooked meat-based stuffing around, even if it is in the refrigerator, for more than 2–3 hours.

Most stuffings are made from a base of fresh breadcrumbs, sausagemeat or other minced meat, rice or suet. Breadcrumbs are best made from a loaf that is 2–3 days old—new bread makes crumbs which are rather too moist. Rice should be cooked and left to cool before adding to a stuffing; it is particularly good in stuffings containing fruit or nuts.

Most stuffings need a little fat, and suet is the one most commonly used. Fresh suet from the butcher has the best flavour, but packet shredded suet is more

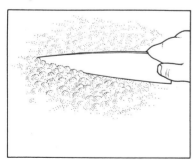

Chopping fresh suet finely

convenient. Chop fresh suet very finely, dusting it with flour to stop it sticking to the knife. Butter is used in some recipes in place of suet, and many people prefer the flavour of a stuffing made with butter if it is to be served cold.

Forcemeat balls

To make forcemeat balls, use any finely minced stuffing mixture. Instead of putting it inside the bird, roll the mixture into small balls. To cook, either roast them round the bird, or fry them separately. Use as a garnish and serve 2–3 balls per person.

CHESTNUT STUFFING

Makes enough for a 4.5 kg (10 lb) turkey

50 g (2 oz) bacon, rinded and chopped

225 g (8 oz) unsweetened chestnut purée

100 g (4 oz) fresh white breadcrumbs

5 ml (1 tsp) chopped parsley

25 g (1 oz) butter or margarine, melted

grated rind of 1 lemon

salt and freshly ground pepper

1 egg, beaten

Fry the bacon gently in its own fat until crisp and drain well on absorbent kitchen paper. Then mix with all the remaining ingredients.

HERB STUFFING

Makes enough for a 1.8 kg (4 lb) chicken

50 g (2 oz) bacon, rinded and chopped

45 ml (3 tbsp) shredded suet

100 g (4 oz) fresh white breadcrumbs

15 ml (1 tbsp) chopped parsley

10 ml (2 tsp) dried mixed herbs or 30 ml (2 tbsp) chopped fresh mixed herbs

grated rind of ½ a lemon

1 small (size 6) egg, beaten

salt and freshly ground pepper

milk or stock, to bind

Fry the bacon in its own fat without browning and drain it on absorbent kitchen paper. Then mix it with the remaining ingredients, moistening with enough milk or stock to bind the mixture.

SAGE AND ONION STUFFING

Makes enough for a 1.8 kg (4 lb) duck. Double the quantities for a goose

2 large onions, skinned and chopped

25 g (1 oz) butter or margarine

salt and freshly ground pepper

100 g (4 oz) fresh white breadcrumbs

10 ml (2 tsp) dried sage

Put the onions in a saucepan and cover with water. Bring to the boil and cook for 10 minutes. Drain and mix with the other ingredients.

SAUSAGE AND APPLE STUFFING

Makes enough for a 4.5 kg (10 lb) turkey

450 g (1 lb) sausagemeat

3 cooking apples, peeled, cored and chopped

1 medium onion, skinned and chopped

2 sticks of celery, trimmed and chopped

225 g (8 oz) fresh white breadcrumbs

2 eggs, beaten

salt and freshly ground pepper

1 Brown the sausagemeat and remove from the pan. Pour off all but 60 ml (4 tbsp) fat.

2 Add the apples, onion and celery and cook for 5–10 minutes until soft. Stir in the sausagemeat and remaining ingredients. Cool before using.

SULTANA AND LEMON STUFFING

Makes enough for a 1.8 kg (4 lb) duck.
Double the quantities for a goose

1 medium onion, skinned and finely chopped
50 g (2 oz) sultanas
150 ml ($\frac{1}{4}$ pint) dry cider
100 g (4 oz) fresh white breadcrumbs
5 ml (1 tsp) grated lemon rind
15 ml (1 tbsp) chopped parsley
salt and freshly ground pepper
1 egg, beaten

1 Put the onion, sultanas and cider into a small saucepan and simmer for 20 minutes, or until the liquid is almost absorbed.

2 Mix with the breadcrumbs, grated lemon rind and parsley and season well with salt and pepper. Bind with the beaten egg.

POTATOES

Various types of potato are traditionally served with poultry, notably roast potatoes, creamed potatoes, game chips and match-stick potatoes. Fried crumbs are served with quail.

Roast potatoes: Using old potatoes, peel in the usual way and cut into even-sized pieces. Cook in salted water for 5–10 minutes—depending on the size—and drain well. Transfer them to a roasting tin containing 100 g (4 oz) of hot lard or chicken fat, baste well and cook in the oven at 220°C (425°F) mark 7 for about 20 minutes; turn them and continue cooking for another 20 minutes, or until soft inside and crisp and brown out-side. Drain well on absorbent kitchen paper and serve in an un-covered serving dish, sprinkled with salt.

If preferred, do not parboil the potatoes to begin with—in this case they will take about 50–60 minutes to cook.

They can also be cooked in the tin around the bird, when little or no extra fat will be needed.

Creamed potatoes: Mash boiled potatoes with a knob of butter, salt and pepper to taste and a little milk. Beat them well over a gentle heat with a wooden spoon until fluffy. Serve in a heated dish, mark with a fork and sprinkle with chopped parsley.

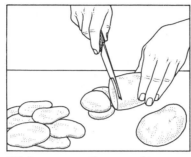

Slicing potatoes for game chips

Game chips: Scrub and peel the potatoes and slice very thinly into rounds. Soak them in cold water, dry and fry in deep fat at 190°C (375°F) for about 3 minutes. Remove and drain on absorbent kitchen paper. Just before serving, reheat the fat and fry the chips again rapidly until crisp and browned. Drain well on absorbent kitchen paper and serve in an un-covered dish, sprinkled with salt.

Matchstick potatoes: Cut potatoes into very small chips of matchstick size. Follow the method for game chips.

Fried crumbs: Fry 50–100 g (2–4 oz) fresh white breadcrumbs in 25 g (1 oz) butter until golden

Making fried breadcrumbs

brown. Stir from time to time to ensure even browning.

TRADITIONAL ACCOMPANIMENTS FOR ROAST POULTRY

Chicken	forcemeat balls
	chipolata sausages
	bacon rolls
	thin gravy
	roast potatoes
Duck	sage and onion stuffing
	fruit stuffing
	apple sauce
	thin gravy
Turkey	forcemeat balls
	chipolata sausages
	bacon rolls
	bread sauce
	cranberry sauce
	watercress
	giblet gravy
Goose	sage and onion stuffing
	apple sauce
	giblet gravy
Guinea Fowl	watercress
	bread sauce
	thin gravy
Quail	croûtes
	thin gravy
	fried crumbs
	matchstick or chipped potatoes

GRAVIES AND SAUCES FOR POULTRY

The best gravies are made with stock based on the giblets, with any bones that are available. After cooking your poultry, never throw away the bones but use them to make a stock for next time; either freeze it or store in the refriger-ator, boiling every 2–3 days.

The lighter meats, such as chicken and guinea fowl, are usually served with a thin gravy, turkey and goose are served with a richer version (see Giblet gravy).

Sauces for poultry may be made with stock or milk, or with a mix-ture of the two.

Thin gravy
Pour the fat very slowly from the roasting tin, draining it off carefully from one corner and leaving the sediment behind. Season well

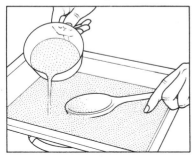

Adding hot stock to roasting tin

and add 300 ml (½ pint) hot stock. Stir thoroughly with a wooden spoon until all the sediment is scraped from the tin and the gravy is a rich brown; return the tin to the heat and boil for 2–3 minutes. Serve very hot.

POULTRY STOCK
Makes about 1.1–1.4 litres (2–2½ pints)

1 carcass, fresh or cooked, with giblets (except liver)

1.4–1.7 litres (2½–3 pints) cold water

1 small onion, skinned and sliced

2 carrots, peeled and sliced

1 stick of celery, sliced

1 bouquet garni

5 ml (1 tsp) salt

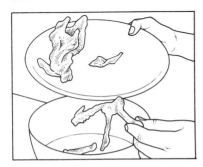

1 Break down the carcass and put it in a large saucepan with the giblets. Add the water and the remaining ingredients.

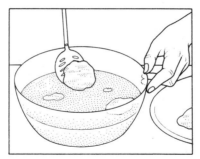

2 Bring to the boil uncovered and remove the scum. Cover and simmer for 3 hours. Strain, and when cold remove all traces of fat from the surface.

Pressure Cooker Method

1 Follow step 1 (see left), using the pressure cooker instead of a saucepan, but reduce the amount of cold water to 1.1 litres (2 pints).

2 Bring to high (15 lb) pressure and cook for 45 minutes if using a cooked carcass, 1 hour if using a fresh carcass. Reduce pressure at room temperature. After cooking finish as above.

GIBLET GRAVY
Makes 600 ml (1 pint)

poultry giblets

1 small onion

1 small carrot, peeled

1 stick of celery, trimmed and cut into chunks

bacon rinds

salt and freshly ground pepper

1.1 litres (2 pints) water

15 ml (1 tbsp) flour

butter

1 Put the gizzard, heart and neck (not the liver) in a saucepan with the vegetables, a few bacon rinds, seasoning and the water. Bring to the boil, cover and simmer for about 2 hours.

2 Strain the giblet stock into a basin. Discard the vegetables and bacon rinds and, if you wish, set aside the cooked giblets for use in another dish.

3 When cooked, remove the bird to a warm plate and pour off most of the fat from the tin, leaving behind sediment and about 30 ml (2 tbsp) fat.

4 Blend the flour into the fat in the roasting tin. Cook until it turns brown, stirring continuously and scraping any sediment from the bottom of the tin. Slowly stir in 600 ml (1 pint) giblet stock. Bring to the boil, stirring.

5 Meanwhile, sauté the liver in a knob of butter until just cooked. Remove from the pan, drain and chop it into small pieces.

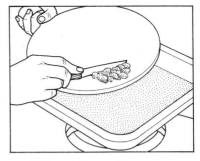

6 Add the chopped liver to the gravy and simmer for 2–3 minutes to heat. Check the seasoning. Pour into a gravy boat and keep hot until needed.

APPLE SAUCE

Makes 300 ml (½ pint)

450 g (1 lb) cooking apples, peeled and cored
30–45 ml (2–3 tbsp) water
25 g (1 oz) butter or margarine
30–60 ml (2–4 tbsp) sugar

1 Slice the apples and put them in a pan with the water. Cook gently for about 10 minutes, until soft. Beat the fruit well, then purée in a blender or press through a sieve.

2 Beat the butter into the mixture and sweeten to taste. Serve with roast duck or goose.

BARBECUE SAUCE

Serves 4

50 g (2 oz) butter or margarine
1 large onion, skinned and chopped
5 ml (1 tsp) tomato purée
30 ml (2 tbsp) vinegar
30 ml (2 tbsp) demerara sugar
10 ml (2 tsp) mustard powder
30 ml (2 tbsp) Worcestershire sauce
150 ml (¼ pint) water

1 Melt the fat in a saucepan and fry the onion for 5 minutes, until soft. Stir in the tomato purée and continue cooking for a further 3 minutes.

2 Blend together the remaining ingredients until smooth and stir in the onion mixture. Return the sauce to the pan and boil uncovered for a further 10 minutes. Serve with chicken.

BÉCHAMEL SAUCE

Makes about 300 ml (½ pint)

300 ml (½ pint) milk
1 small onion, skinned and quartered
1 small carrot, peeled and sliced
½ small stick of celery, trimmed and sliced
2 cloves
6 white peppercorns
1 blade of mace
1 sprig of parsley
1 sprig of thyme
1 bay leaf
25 g (1 oz) butter or margarine
25 g (1 oz) flour
salt and freshly ground pepper

1 Put the milk into a saucepan with the onion, carrot, celery, cloves, peppercorns, mace, parsley, thyme and bay leaf. Slowly bring just to the boil, then remove from the heat and cover the pan. Set aside to infuse for 30 minutes. Strain, reserving the flavoured milk.

2 Melt the fat in a saucepan. Stir in the flour and cook gently for 2 minutes, stirring. Do not allow the mixture to brown. Remove the pan from the heat and gradually stir in the flavoured milk.

3 Bring to the boil and continue to cook, stirring, until the sauce thickens. Simmer very gently for 3 minutes. Remove from the heat and season with salt and pepper.

BREAD SAUCE

Makes about 450 ml (¾ pint)

2 cloves
1 medium onion, skinned
450 ml (¾ pint) milk
salt
few peppercorns
½ small bay leaf
knob of butter
75 g (3 oz) fresh white breadcrumbs

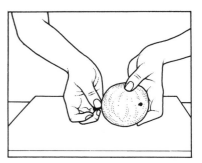

1 Stick the cloves into the onion and put it into a saucepan with the milk, salt, peppercorns and bay leaf. Bring almost to the boil, then leave covered in a warm place for 20 minutes.

2 Remove the peppercorns and bay leaf. Add the butter and breadcrumbs and cook very slowly for about 15 minutes, stirring from time to time. Remove the onion. Serve with turkey or guinea fowl.

CRANBERRY SAUCE

Makes about 450 ml (¾ pint)

225 g (8 oz) sugar
300 ml (½ pint) water
225 g (8 oz) cranberries
port (optional)

1 Put the sugar and water in a saucepan and dissolve the sugar over gentle heat, then boil for 5 minutes.

2 Add the cranberries and a little port if you wish. Simmer gently for 10 minutes, or until the berries burst. Cool before serving. Serve with roast turkey.

CURRANT-MINT JELLY

Makes about 225 ml (8 fl oz)

250–350 g (10–12 oz) redcurrant jelly
30 ml (2 tbsp) grated orange rind
30 ml (2 tbsp) chopped fresh mint or 10 ml (2 tsp) dried mint

Mix all the ingredients, stirring until well blended. Serve with hot or cold roast poultry.

INDEX

159